Social Issues
in Literature

DATE DUE

Class Conflict in
F. Scott Fitzgerald's
The Great Gatsby

Other Books in the Social Issues in Literature Series:

Racism in Maya Angelou's *I Know Why the Caged Bird Sings*

Racism in Harper Lee's *To Kill a Mockingbird*

Women's Issues in Amy Tan's *The Joy Luck Club*

Social Issues in Literature

Class Conflict in F. Scott Fitzgerald's *The Great Gatsby*

Claudia Johnson, Book Editor

GREENHAVEN PRESS
A part of Gale, Cengage Learning

GALE
CENGAGE Learning

Detroit • New York • San Francisco • New Haven, Conn • Waterville, Maine • London

Christine Nasso, *Publisher*
Elizabeth Des Chenes, *Managing Editor*

© 2008 Greenhaven Press, a part of Gale, Cengage Learning.

For more information, contact:
Greenhaven Press
27500 Drake Rd.
Farmington Hills, MI 48331-3535
Or you can visit our Internet site at gale.cengage.com

Articles in Greenhaven Press anthologies are often edited for length to meet page requirements. In addition, original titles of these works are changed to clearly present the main thesis and to explicitly indicate the author's opinion. Every effort is made to ensure that Greenhaven Press accurately reflects the original intent of the authors. Every effort has been made to trace the owners of copyrighted material.

Cover photograph reproduced by permission of Topical Press Agency/Getty Images.

ISBN-13: 978-0-7377-3899-5 (hardcover)
ISBN-10: 0-7377-3899-5 (hardcover)
ISBN-13: 978-0-7377-3903-9 (pbk.)
ISBN-10: 0-7377-3903-7 (pbk.)

Library of Congress Control Number: 2007938437

Printed in the United States of America
2 3 4 5 6   15 14 13 12 11
FD186

Contents

Introduction   9

Chronology   12

Chapter 1: Background on F. Scott Fitzgerald

1. The Life of F. Scott Fitzgerald   16

Scott Donaldson

Fitzgerald felt like an outsider, on the edges of polite society, whether he was in the local academy, Princeton, or New York.

2. Fitzgerald's View of Class and the American Dream   23

Marius Bewley

Gatsby is an attack on the American Dream as it had degenerated after World War I, a dream which Gatsby, nevertheless, pursues.

Chapter 2: *The Great Gatsby* and Class Conflict

1. The Class Consumerism of Fitzgerald's Life   31

Malcolm Cowley

Cowley prepares the reader of *The Great Gatsby* with details of poverty and class consciousness in F. Scott Fitzgerald's early life.

2. Class Snobbery and Education   36

Scott Donaldson

Fitzgerald's life at Princeton, and Princeton's official reaction to Fitzgerald right up to the late 1960s, demonstrate class snobbishness.

3. World War I and Class   45

James H. Meredith

Gatsby's status as a lieutenant in the war provides him temporary access to upper-class society, despite his humble beginnings.

4. Upper- and Middle-Class Waste
   and Destruction   53
   Kirk Curnutt

   The nouveau riche attempt to climb socially by accumulating things rather than by talent and character.

5. The Universality of Class Divisions   60
   A.E. Dyson

   Gatsby is the portrait of a broken society, where the upper class exploits those beneath them, living covered in dust and ashes.

6. Two American Dreams in Conflict   67
   Brian M. Barbour

   Barbour enlarges on the conflicts between readings of the novel as romantic or symbolic and readings that affirm its realism.

7. A Corruption of Character   73
   Michael Millgate

   Fitzgerald, as a social novelist, focuses on the upper class, highlighting both the desire and the repulsion they elicit.

8. A Flawed View of Greatness   80
   Ronald Berman

   Fitzgerald's characters have relinquished responsibility, obligation, and concern for community in exchange for status.

9. Daisy, Jordan, and Myrtle   88
   Rena Sanderson

   Fitzgerald is attracted to and disgusted with the woman of the 1920s, an image that he himself has frequently been credited with creating.

10. Genteel Women and Flappers   93
    Elizabeth Kaspar Aldrich

    A constant topic of Fitzgerald's writing is the modeling of his heroines on his wife Zelda, a careless but ambitious upper-class woman.

11. Class and Spiritual Corruption   97

John W. Bicknell

For some readers *Gatsby* is a confirmation that society
can be improved; others may see the inevitable destruction of civilization.

12. Humor in the Service of Class Criticism   101

Robert Roulston

This is a radical reading of Fitzgerald's novel as a humorous comedy, with Buchanan playing the greatest arrogant buffoon.

13. The Illusion of Class   108

Tom Burnam

Gatsby shows that the elegance of the upper class is
built upon ashes and shifting sand—an illusion of order
in chaos.

14. Daisy or Marx?   113

Ronald J. Gervais

Fitzgerald was continually torn between the aristocracy
and a Marxist dream of social equality and justice.

Chapter 3: Contemporary Perspectives on Class Conflict

1. The Rich Are Different   120

Richard Conniff

In a funny comment on the rich upper class, the wealthy
are compared to animals.

2. Twenty-First-Century Flappers   128

Gloria Goodale

Fitzgerald's upper-class materialistic celebrity flapper
continues in the careless life of Paris Hilton and her
friends.

3. The Criminal Class   133

Gene Mustain and Jerry Capeci

John Gotti, like Gatsby, made his money illegally and by
corrupting society. Both spent their money lavishly on
clothes and cars.

4. The Club and Class   **139**
   Mike Morris

   The obsession with the rank one finds in university social clubs is just as frantic now as it was in Fitzgerald's
   days at Princeton.

For Further Discussion   **145**

For Further Reading   **146**

Bibliography   **147**

Index   **150**

Introduction

The American Dream, articulated by such Founding Fathers as Benjamin Franklin, held out the possibility of equality and an escape from the inevitable poverty of the Old World where, for centuries, a rigid aristocracy had kept the lower classes in what were believed to be their God-intended places. In the New World, titles had been abolished; class divisions eased, and the poor had the opportunity to own land and better their social standing.

After World War I, all classes lost much of their sense of social responsibility as the old Puritanism died out. Many members of a class that once saw itself as being responsible to a standard of morality began turning to pleasure and recklessness.

Virtually everything F. Scott Fitzgerald wrote contains an inherent consciousness of class struggle. Though in "May Day" he tackled labor struggles, in *The Great Gatsby*, except for the Wilsons, he did little to analyze the majority of the population in the twenties, who worked with their hands, many of whom struggled to survive and were abused for their own pursuit of the American Dream.

Still, in *Gatsby*, (and in his other fiction), while he focuses on the upper ranks of society, he provides his readers with glimpses of several social classes. At the top of the pyramid are the Buchanans who secured their wealth by inheritance, rather than work, and Nick Carraway, also an aristocrat, who used contacts to find himself a position on Wall Street. Then there are the crude, rough, newly rich who appear at Gatsby's parties. This upper-middle-class group is as high in society as the humbly born Gatsby can climb, despite the green light far at the end of the Buchanans' pier, continually beckoning him. Neither his ill-gotten money, his charm, nor his connections allow him to rise beyond the mercantile upper-middle class.

Finally, the readers get bleak glimpses of the lower-class Wilsons, living above a mechanic's garage in a wasteland covered in dust and ashes. In exchange for being Tom Buchanan's mistress, Myrtle Wilson is provided with an apartment where she gives parties that are unconscious parodies of upper-middle- and upper-class galas. A billboard with a pair of cold eyes looks out over it all like an uncaring god.

The Great Gatsby echoes the importance of rank in many of Fitzgerald's works and in Fitzgerald's own life. A young man of refinement and ambition is devoted to and struggling for the American Dream—the topmost, beautiful place in the exclusive upper class, represented by a beautiful woman.

Nick and Gatsby and Fitzgerald himself were all middle westerners at a time when social success, they imagined, could only be found in New York City. So Gatsby and Fitzgerald, in pursuit of the American Dream, made their pilgrimage, leaving their Midwestern working-class roots behind them and entering a post–World War I adolescent society, where money buys pleasure and self-aggrandizement. But the reader perceives that, ultimately, Gatsby's dream is a nightmare, an illusion bound to destroy him.

Fitzgerald experienced the same social rejection that Gatsby did and in some ways his background was very like Gatsby's. The loss of family money left the Fitzgeralds on the fringes of society in St. Paul, Minnesota. They were never completely considered part of the upper-class group, though they could point to an illustrious family member in their background—Francis Scott Key—for whom Scott Fitzgerald was named. Still the outsider, Scott, nevertheless, attended prestigious academies. Being accepted by Princeton was a dream come true for the socially conscious Scott. But Princeton students looked down on him, and his performance as a student was unacceptable. Only a small exclusive literary and theatrical group welcomed him to join them.

Fitzgerald worked hard to improve his station in society, making a living as a writer of fiction for magazines and, then, writing novels, most of which painted a picture of a certain bizarre segment of 1920s society, known as the Jazz Age. No other writer captured the Jazz Age as Fitzgerald was able to do. He was often said to have even invented the Jazz Age with its outrageous flappers, reckless young men, and gangsterism.

But Fitzgerald was also met with rejection among another class—his fellow writers and critics. H.L. Mencken, the most important literary critic at the time Fitzgerald was writing, pronounced *The Great Gatsby* to be shallow and silly. Ernest Hemingway's comments were so withering that Hemingway felt compelled to apologize.

Despite being constantly belittled by the upper ranks of society and literary figures, Fitzgerald continued in works like *Gatsby* to appear ambiguous in his approach to class, a problem that critics still puzzle over. For while he savages the upper-class, like the Buchanans, for being snobbish, heartless, and destructive, he gives the inevitable impression in most of his work, especially *Gatsby*, that he is also attracted to them and wants to be a part of those tasteful surroundings and carefree opulence—something that appears on the surface to be cool, serene, and secure.

The following articles, stressing the corruption of the American Dream, are analyses of class as Fitzgerald portrays it in *The Great Gatsby*.

Chronology

1896

Francis Scott Key Fitzgerald is born on September 24 in St. Paul, Minnesota.

1898

Business losses lead the Fitzgeralds to move to several different locations, seeking an adequate income.

1908

The Fitzgerald family returns to St. Paul. In the same year, Scott enters St. Paul Academy.

1911

Fitzgerald enters a prep school, the Newman School, in Hackensack, New Jersey, continuing the writing he had begun at St. Paul's.

1913

Fitzgerald enrolls at Princeton University. His academic performance is poor and, while he is successful in some of his playwriting attempts, he never graduates.

26 October 1917

Fitzgerald joins the army as a second lieutenant.

1918

Fitzgerald is transferred to an army base near Montgomery, Alabama, where he meets Southern belle Zelda Sayre.

1919

Fitzgerald begins working for an advertising agency in New York City and continues writing fiction for magazines. He returns to St. Paul later in the year to work on his first novel, trying to prove to Zelda that he can make sufficient money to support her.

1920

Fitzgerald publishes his first novel, *This Side of Paradise*, and he and Zelda marry.

1922

Fitzgerald's second novel, *The Beautiful and the Damned*, is published in book form. He and Zelda move to an expensive neighborhood in Great Neck, Long Island.

1924–1937

Fitzgerald and Zelda spend most of their time in Europe.

1925

The Great Gatsby is published.

1930

Zelda's escalating mental problems cause her to be hospitalized in a clinic outside Paris.

1931

The Fitzgeralds return to the United States where Zelda is hospitalized on and off.

1932

Zelda sees her novel, *Save Me the Waltz*, into print.

1934

Fitzgerald's *Tender Is the Night* is published in book form.

1936

Zelda is hospitalized in Asheville, North Carolina, where she remains for most of the rest of her life, dying in a fire there in 1948.

1937

Fitzgerald begins spending time in Hollywood, hoping to make money writing for the movies. He meets Sheilah Graham, a gossip columnist and has a romantic relationship with her for the rest of his life.

1939

Fitzgerald begins treatment for alcoholism from which he has suffered most of his life.

1940

Fitzgerald dies on December 21 of a heart attack.

1941

Fitzgerald's unfinished novel, *The Last Tycoon*, is edited by his friend Edmund Wilson, and published.

Social Issues
in Literature

CHAPTER 1

Background on
F. Scott Fitzgerald

The Life of F. Scott Fitzgerald

Scott Donaldson

Scott Donaldson was for many years the Louisa Colley Professor of English at the College of William and Mary. His books include The Cambridge Companion to Hemingway *(1996) and* Hemingway vs. Fitzgerald *(2001).*

Although Fitzgerald had not found in St. Paul, Minnesota, where he spent his teen years, the same class divisions that could be found in the South and the Northeast, he and his family were well aware of their marginalized position on the outskirts of polite society. From the time he was a boy, the author was also sensitive to the class standing of the girls and young women he met. He courted girls who came from families in high social brackets—from the Southern belles he met while stationed in the army in the South, to a wealthy Chicago debutante whose father dismissed him as too poor to marry his daughter. These elements of Fitzgerald's personal ambition—to have money, to be embraced by upper-class society, and to secure a wife of social distinction—form part of the background of The Great Gatsby.

F. Scott Fitzgerald was a writer very much of his own time.... His own career followed the pattern of the nation, booming in the early 1920s and skidding into near oblivion during the depths of the Depression. Yet his fiction did more than merely report on his times, or on himself as a prototypical representative, for Fitzgerald had the gift of double vision. Like Walt Whitman or his own Nick Carraway, he was simultaneously within and without, at once immersed in his times and able to view them—and himself—with striking objectivity. This rare ability, along with his rhetorical brilliance, has established Fitzgerald as one of the major novelists and story writers of the twentieth century.

Scott Donaldson, "F. Scott Fitzgerald," *Dictionary of Literary Biography.* Farmington Hills, MI: Gale Research Company, 1981. Copyright © 1985 Gale Research Company. Reproduced by permission of Gale, a part of Cengage Learning.

Scott Fitzgerald's Family Background

The source of Fitzgerald's talent remains a mystery. Edward Fitzgerald, his father, came from "tired, old stock" with roots in Maryland. His job with Proctor and Gamble took the family to Buffalo and Syracuse for most of his son's first decade. Then the company let Edward Fitzgerald go, and he returned to Saint Paul blaming no one but himself and going daily to an office where there was not much for him to do. He drank more than he should have but had beautiful manners that he taught to his only son. Edward Fitzgerald's great-great-grandfather was the brother of Francis Scott Key's grandfather, and if Scott Fitzgerald claimed a closer relationship, it was hardly his fault. He had after all been christened Francis Scott Key Fitzgerald, and his mother Mollie was inordinately proud of the Key connection she had married into. Her own family could offer no pretensions to aristocracy, certainly. Philip Francis McQuillan, her father, had emigrated from Ireland in 1843 and built a substantial wholesale grocery business in Saint Paul. From him may have stemmed the energy that fueled Scott Fitzgerald's production of 160 stories and four and a half novels. Equally important, probably, was Fitzgerald's sense of having come from two widely different Celtic strains. He had early developed an inferiority complex in a family where the "black Irish half . . . had the money and looked down on the Maryland side of the family who had, and really had . . . 'breeding.'" As a boy Scott used to imagine that he was born of royal blood but had turned up on the Fitzgeralds' doorstep. He loved his father, but could hardly respect him. His feelings about his mother were even more complicated. . . .

Poor Boys and Rich Girls

During the hectic party season in Saint Paul, Christmas of his sophomore year at Princeton, Fitzgerald more than met his match in the charming Ginevra King of Chicago, Lake Forest, and the great world of wealth and family background. They dated a few times and conducted a long and heated correspondence, but in the end, almost inevitably, Fitzgerald lost her. There is a legend that Ginevra's father told Scott that "poor boys shouldn't think of marrying rich girls." . . .

Love Affair

Fitzgerald wrote *The Great Gatsby* in France, where he and his wife and daughter were to spend most of the last half of the 1920s. The novel bears almost no resemblance in form to those that had come before. In Jay Gatsby, nee James Gatz, Fitzgerald created far more than just another Amory Blaine seeking his fortune in the world, for in his misguided romantic way Gatsby stands for a deeper malaise in the culture—a sickness that drives young men to think that riches can obliterate the past and capture the hearts of the girls of their dreams. Gatsby's dream girl, hardly worthy of his romantic quest, is Daisy Fay Buchanan, wife to the safely (not newly) rich Tom Buchanan. She and Gatsby had met and fallen in love during the war, when Jay was a young officer with no money or position: "eventually he took Daisy one still October night, took her because he had no real right to touch her hand.

"He might have despised himself, for he had certainly taken her under false pretenses. I don't mean that he had traded on his phantom millions, but he had deliberately given Daisy a sense of security; he let her believe that he was a person from much the same stratum as herself—that he was fully able to take care of her. As a matter of fact, he had no such facilities—he had no comfortable family standing behind him, and he was liable at the whim of an impersonal government to be blown anywhere about the world.

"But he didn't despise himself and it didn't turn out as he had imagined. He had intended, probably, to take what he could and go—but now he found that he had committed himself to the following of a grail. He knew that Daisy was extraordinary, but he didn't realize just how extraordinary a 'nice' girl could be. She vanished into her rich house, into her rich, full life, leaving Gatsby—nothing. He felt married to her, that was all." When he went overseas, she married Buchanan. The novel tells the story of his attempt to get Daisy back some four years later. In the meantime he has made a great deal of money, partly from bootlegging liquor; Daisy has borne a daughter; and Tom has taken as his mistress Myrtle Wilson, the wife of the owner of a garage in the ash heaps that lie along the road about halfway between West Egg and Manhattan. Told so baldly, the novel sounds like material for the pulps. But the story is not told that way at all, but through the informing intelligence of Nick Carraway, an almost perfect narrator.

Clearly, Fitzgerald had been reading Joseph Conrad and discovered in his use of the character Marlow as teller of the tale a way of distancing himself from his story without sacrificing intensity. Nick Carraway functions as an ideal Marlow in *The Great Gatsby*, for he is connected by background to the Buchanans (Daisy is his cousin, he had been at Yale with Tom) and by proximity to Gatsby (he rents a small house near Gatsby's garish mansion), and he has—he tells us—cultivated the habit of withholding judgments. Nick does not particularly like Tom, even to begin with, but he knows and understands Tom and his milieu. At first, Gatsby is a mystery to Nick. He spends too ostentatiously and entertains too lavishly. Besides giving parties, Gatsby wears pink suits, drives yellow cars, and is in business with the man who fixed the World Series. Yet before the tragic end—when in a case of mistaken identity for which Tom and Daisy Buchanan are jointly responsible, Myrtle Wilson's husband kills Gatsby—Nick comes to see that the Buchanans were "careless people . . . who smashed up things and creatures and then retreated back into their money or their vast carelessness, or whatever it was that kept them together, and let other people clean up the mess,"

F. Scott Fitzgerald, his wife Zelda Sayre, and their daughter Scottie are pictured in their apartment in Paris on July 16, 1925. AP Images.

and he realizes that Gatsby, the bootlegger who followed his dream, was "worth the whole damn bunch put together." Coming from Carraway, no saint himself and a bit of a snob, a man who "disapproved" of Gatsby from beginning to end as he would disapprove of any other parvenu [newcomer to wealth], that judgment takes on absolute authority.

The Careless Class

Gatsby's greatness lies in his capacity for illusion. Had he seen Daisy for what she was, he could not have loved her with such single-minded devotion. He comes to recapture Daisy, and for a time it looks as though he will succeed. But he must inevitably fail, because of his inability to separate the ideal from the real. Everything he has done, and it is clear that much of what he has done is on the shady side of the law, Gatsby has done in order to present himself as worthy of Daisy. By crassly materialistic ends he hopes to capture the ideal girl. Toward the end, Nick reflects, Gatsby must have realized that Daisy was not the golden girl after all, that she too had sprung from the material world and was made of all-too-human stuff, but those are Nick's thoughts, not necessarily Gatsby's. For all Fitzgerald lets us know, Gatsby dies with his dream intact, and then it is left to Nick to arrange for the service and erase the dirty word from the steps of Gatsby's house and clean up the mess.

Though hundreds had come to Gatsby's parties, hardly anyone comes to his funeral. His father is there, a shiftless and uneducated man who even while standing in his son's mansion prefers to admire the photograph of that mansion. So is Owl Eyes, who had been startled to find that the books in Gatsby's library were real, even though their pages were uncut. Like the books Gatsby was the real thing, but unformed, unlettered, and for all his financial cunning, ignorant. Like his father he preferred the picture in his mind to mundane reality. *The Great Gatsby* abounds in touches like these.

The Great Gatsby has inspired probably as much critical commentary as any other twentieth-century American novel, but it is so intricately patterned and tightly knit, so beautifully integrated through a series of parallels, that it hardly seems possible that criticism will exhaust the novel. If *This Side of Paradise* resembles the Wellsian novel of saturation, where everything is included, *The Great Gatsby* epitomizes the Jamesian novel of selection, where every detail fits and nothing is superfluous. It's the kind of novel—and there aren't many—that gets better each time one rereads it.

The reviews for *The Great Gatsby* were the most favorable so far. Most notably Gilbert Seldes proclaimed that Fitzgerald "has mastered his talents and gone soaring in a beautiful flight, leaving behind him everything dubious and tricky in his earlier work, and leaving even further behind all the men of his own generation and most of his elders." He praises Fitzgerald's ability to report on a "a tiny section of life . . . with irony and pity and a consuming passion," calling the novel "passionate . . . , with such an abundance of feeling for the characters (feeling their integral reality, not hating or loving them objectively) that the most trivial of the actors in the drama are endowed with vitality," and he also recognizes that Fitzgerald's characters "become universal also. He has now something of extreme importance to say; and it is good fortune for us that he knows how to say it."

Fitzgerald's View of Class and the American Dream

Marius Bewley

Marius Bewley, one of the most prominent critics in the history of American literature, ended his career as a distinguished professor of English at Rutgers University. He regularly reviewed for prestigious periodicals, including the New York Times *and the* Hudson Review. *His study of Fitzgerald,* The Eccentric Design, *permanently changed the way that critics looked at the author.*

Fitzgerald's work, more than that of any other American writer, is based on the dual concepts of class and the American dream. The Great Gatsby *illustrates the ways in which the emergence of conspicuous consumption has corrupted the historic values of America and is an exploration of the changing boundaries between material success and social acceptance.*

More than with any other writer in the American tradition, Scott Fitzgerald's novels have been based on a concept of class. In this respect he far exceeds [Henry] James, whose characters, if they belong to an upper class, belong to one which is . . . , strangely disembodied, and not really related to any economic structure at all—at least until his late years. Even then, the recognition was one of pained, shrinking, and rather superficial acknowledgement. The class role of Fitzgerald's characters is possible because he instinctively realized the part that money played in creating and supporting a way of life focused in the Ivy League universities, country clubs, trips to the Riviera, and the homes of the wealthy. He is the first American writer who seems to have discovered that

Marius Bewley, from *The Eccentric Design: Form in the Classic American Novel*. London: Chatto & Windus, 1959. Copyright © 1959 Marius Bewley. Reprinted by permission of The Random House Group Ltd.

such a thing as American class *really* existed—American class as an endemic growth, to be distinguished from James's delightfully mild Newport cosmopolities, united in the common circumstance of their having more or less lived in Europe. Fitzgerald was enabled to make this discovery because he was almost preternaturally aware of the reality that gold lent to the play of appearances he loved so much. Because he immersed himself so completely in this play of appearances—in swank parties, jazz tunes, alcohol, and coloured lights—many have questioned the fineness and discrimination of his intelligence. But what he immersed himself in *was* the America of his time (and almost as much, perhaps, of ours), and just because he was as intelligent as any of the novelists treated here, he ended by making an evaluation of the life and wealth he seemed to love that was deeper, more richly informed, and at least as sensitive, as any ever made by James. The charge that Fitzgerald was 'taken in' by wealth is as irritating as it is untrue. There is a radical difference between coveting a 'tony' life that can only be supported by money—lots of money—and being critically and morally unable to assess the conditions under which the money must be acquired or its ultimate effects on character. As an artist, Scott Fitzgerald knew the worst there was to know about all these things, and he knew it with an inwardness and a profoundness. . . .

I said that Scott Fitzgerald was the first of the great American writers to have found that a 'treatable' class, with its accompanying manners, really did exist in America—to have found it sufficiently, at any rate, to have been able to create characters who are representative of a socially solid and defined group rather than symbolic embodiments of the ultimate American solitude, or two-dimensional figures in the American morality play. As I shall point out later, Gatsby is an exception to this. He is a mythic embodiment in the great American tradition of Natty Bumppo and Huck Finn and Ishmael; but Fitzgerald's stories are populated by a type of rich or popular young man who, in a way that never really had happened in American literature before, carries a weight of representativeness. His manners, attitudes, and ideals, are shared by a large and important group, and have the admiring support of the influential members of the older generation. One may not like the group; its civilization may be a far cry from what one finds in Jane Austen's class structure (perhaps not if one looks into the fortunes of the great Whig peers who stood at the top of that structure), but one has to admit its existence, and its demands for 'treatment'. As the class had its origins in wealth, as its manners and way of life were nourished by gold, it was Fitzgerald's sense of, his feeling for, money, that enabled him not only to appreciate the surfaces, but to penetrate to the heart of the structure. But if that had been all it would certainly not have been enough. If Scott Fitzgerald loved wealth he was not taken in by it, and some of his gaudiest celebrations of it are simultaneously the most annihilating criticisms. . . .

A History of the American Dream

I should like to pause for a moment's reflection on just what, historically, this American dream is.

Essentially, the phrase represents the romantic enlargement of the possibilities of life on a level at which the material and the spiritual have become inextricably confused. As such, it led inevitably towards the problem that has always confronted American artists dealing with American experience—the problem of determining the hidden boundary in the American vision of life at which the reality ends and the illusion begins. Historically, the American dream is anti-Calvinistic—in rejecting man's tainted nature it is even anti-Christian. It believes in the goodness of nature and man. It is accordingly a product of the frontier and the West rather than of the New England and Puritan traditions. Youth of the spirit—youth of the body as well—is a requirement of its existence, limit and deprivation are its blackest devils. But it shows an astonishing incapacity to believe in them. . . .

That is the hard kernel, the seed from which the American dream would grow into unpruned luxuriance, to become brutalized at last under the grossly acquisitive spirit of the Gilded Age and Republican capitalism. . . .

In *The Great Gatsby*, the tawdry romance with Daisy, as we shall see, is the means Fitzgerald uses to show Gatsby the intolerable cheapness of his dream and illusion. Fitzgerald has sometimes been criticized for the inadequacy of his treatment of love, but on this point it would be difficult to find any writer in the American tradition who has treated the subject better, or even as well. . . .

The Dying American Dreams

The Great Gatsby is an exploration of the American dream as it exists in a corrupt period, and it is an attempt to determine that concealed boundary that divides the reality from the illusions. The illusions seem more real than the reality itself. Embodied in the subordinate characters in the novel, they threaten to invade the whole of the picture. On the other hand, the reality is embodied in Gatsby; and as opposed to the hard, tangible illusions, the reality is a thing of the spirit, a promise rather than the possession of a vision, a faith in the half-glimpsed, but hardly understood, possibilities of life. In Gatsby's America, the reality is undefined to itself. . . .

Gatsby never succeeds in seeing through the sham of his world or his acquaintances very clearly. It is of the essence of his romantic American vision that it should lack the seasoned powers of discrimination. But it invests those illusions with its own faith, and thus it discovers its projected goodness in the frauds of its crippled world. *The Great Gatsby* becomes the acting out of the tragedy of the American vision. It is a vision totally untouched by the scales of values that order life in a society governed by traditional manners; and Fitzgerald knows

F. Scott Fitzgerald pictured with his wife Zelda Sayre in 1921. Hulton/Archive. Getty Images.

that although it would be easy to condemn and 'place' the illusions by invoking these outside values, to do so would be to kill the reality that lies beyond them, but which can sometimes only be reached through them.

For example, Fitzgerald perfectly understood the inadequacy of Gatsby's romantic view of wealth. But that is not the point. He presents it in Gatsby as a romantic baptism of desire for a reality that stubbornly remains out of his sight. It is as if a savage islander, suddenly touched with Grace, transcended in his prayers and aspirations the grotesque little fetish in which he imagined he discovered the object of his longing. The scene in which Gatsby shows his stacks of beautiful imported shirts to Daisy and Nick has been mentioned as a failure of Gatsby's, and so of Fitzgerald's, critical control of values. Actually, the shirts are sacramentals, and it is clear that Gatsby shows them, neither in vanity nor in pride, but with a reverential humility in the presence of some inner vision he cannot consciously grasp, but toward which he desperately struggles in the only way he knows. . . .

We recognize that the great achievement of this novel is that it manages, while poetically evoking a sense of the goodness of that early dream, to offer the most damaging criticism of it in American literature. The astonishing thing is that the criticism—if indictment wouldn't be the better word—manages to be part of the tribute. Gatsby, the 'mythic' embodiment of the American dream, is shown to us in all his immature romanticism. His insecure grasp of social and human values, his lack of critical intelligence and self-knowledge, his blindness to the pitfalls that surround him in American society, his compulsive optimism, are realized in the text with rare assurance and understanding. And yet the very grounding of these deficiencies is Gatsby's goodness and faith in life, his compelling desire to realize all the possibilities of existence, his belief that we can have an Earthly Paradise populated by Buchanans. A great part of Fitzgerald's achievement is that he suggests effectively that these terrifying deficiencies are not so much the private deficiencies of Gatsby, but are deficiencies inherent in contemporary manifestations of the American vision itself—a vision no doubt admirable, but stupidly defenceless before the equally American world of Tom and Daisy. Gatsby's deficiencies of intelligence and judgment bring him to his tragic death—a death that is spiritual as well as physical. But the more important question that faces us through our sense of the immediate tragedy is where they have brought America.

Social Issues in Literature

CHAPTER 2

The Great Gatsby and Class Conflict

The Class Consumerism
of Fitzgerald's Life

Malcolm Cowley

Malcolm Cowley was a part of the post–World War I Paris group of writers that included Gertrude Stein and Ernest Hemingway. He later became the literary editor of the New Republic. *He was also literary advisor to the Viking Press, where he edited portable editions of the works of Hemingway, Faulkner, and Hawthorne. Cowley, who was famous for his commitment to leftist politics, died in March 1989.*

Fitzgerald followed in his own life the commercial culture he celebrated and deplored in The Great Gatsby. *The generation that emerged from World War I idolized the concepts of money-making and mass consumption. In order to survive financially, Fitzgerald worked for a time in the business world as an advertising copywriter. His income allowed him to live modestly, but without offering him encouragement toward realizing his dream of becoming a successful writer. His walls, for instance, were hung with rejection slips. Finally, however, his sales of fiction to magazines picked up, bringing him enough money to marry Zelda Sayre and join the mass of American consumers. Fitzgerald longed, like many artists, for foreign travel, fine food, and luxury but, unlike them, he concentrated throughout his career on maintaining close ties with the business world.*

Scott . . . said, "America was going on the greatest, gaudiest spree in history and there was going to be plenty to tell about it." There is still plenty to tell about it, in the light of a new age that continues to be curious about the 1920s and usually misjudges them. The gaudiest spree in history was also a moral revolt, and beneath the revolt were social transformations. The 1920s were the age when puritanism was under attack, with the Protestant churches losing their dominant position. They were the age when the country ceased to be English and Scottish and when the children of later immigrations moved forward to take their places in the national life. Theodore Dreiser, whom Fitzgerald regarded as the greatest living American writer, was South German Catholic by descent, H. L. Mencken, the most influential critic, was North German Protestant, and Fitzgerald did not forget for a moment that one side of his own family was "straight potato-famine Irish." Most of his heroes have Irish names and all except Gatsby are city-bred, thus reflecting another social change. The 1920s were the age when American culture became urban instead of rural and when New York set the social and intellectual standards of the country, while its own standards were being set by transplanted Southerners and Midwesterners like Zelda and Scott.

A Gaudy Age

More essentially the 1920s were the age when a production ethic—of saving and self-denial in order to accumulate capital for new enterprises—gave way to a consumption ethic that was needed to provide markets for the new commodities that streamed from the production lines. Instead of being exhorted to save money, more and more of it, people were being exhorted in a thousand ways to buy, enjoy, use once and throw away, in order to buy a later and more expensive model. They followed the instructions, with the result that more goods were produced and consumed or wasted and money was easier to earn or borrow than ever in the past. Foresight went out of fashion. "The Jazz Age," Fitzgerald was to say, "now raced along under its own power, served by great filling stations full of money. . . . Even when you were broke you didn't worry about money, because it was in such profusion around you." . . .

Money Is Virtue

There was one respect in which Fitzgerald, much as he regarded himself as a representative figure of the age, was completely different from most of its serious writers. In that respect he was, as I said, much closer to the men of his college years who were trying to get ahead in the business world; like them he was fascinated by the process of earning and spending money. The young businessmen of his time, much more than those of a later generation, had been taught to measure success, failure, and even virtue in pecuniary terms. They had learned in school and Sunday school that virtue was rewarded with money and vice punished by the loss of money; apparently their one aim should be to earn lots of it fast. Yet money was only a convenient and inadequate symbol for what they dreamed of earning. . . .

In his attitude toward money he revealed the new spirit of an age when conspicuous accumulation was giving way to conspicuous earning and spending. It was an age when gold was melted down and became fluid; when wealth was no longer measured in possessions—land, houses, livestock, machinery—but rather in dollars per year, as a stream is measured by its flow; when for the first time the expenses of government were being met by income taxes more than by property and excise taxes; and when the new tax structure was making it somewhat more difficult to accumulate a stable and lasting fortune. Such fortunes still existed at the hardly accessible peak of the social system, which young men dreamed of reaching like Alpinists, but the romantic figures of the age were not capitalists properly speaking. They were salaried executives and advertising men, they were promoters, salesmen, stock gamblers, or racketeers, and they were millionaires in a new sense—not men each of whom owned a million dollars' worth of property, but men who lived in rented apartments and had nothing but stock certificates and insurance policies

Robert Redford played the role of Jay Gatsby and Mia Farrow the role of Daisy Buchanan in the 1974 film adaptation of The Great Gatsby. © Paramount Pictures/Getty Images.

(or nothing but credit and the right connections), while spending more than the income of the old millionaires.

The change went deep into the texture of American society and deep into the feelings of Americans as individuals. Fitzgerald is its most faithful recorder, not only in the stories that earned him a place in the new high-income class, but also in his personal confessions. . . .

The Lower Classes

In *The Great Gatsby* he must have been thinking about the lower levels of American society when he described the valley of ashes between West Egg and New York—"A fantastic farm," he calls it, "where ashes grow like wheat into ridges and hills and grotesque gardens; where ashes take the forms of houses and chimneys and rising smoke and, finally, with a transcendent effort, of men who move dimly and always crumbling through the powdery air." One of his early titles for the novel was "Among Ash Heaps and Millionaires"—as if he were setting the two against each other while suggesting a vague affinity between them. Tom Buchanan, the brutalized millionaire, finds a mistress in the valley of ashes.

In Fitzgerald's stories there can be no real struggle between this dimly pictured ash-gray proletariat and the bourgeoisie. . . .

The Careless Rich

In *The Great Gatsby*, Tom and Daisy Buchanan would also sacrifice some of their best friends. "They were careless people, Tom and Daisy—they smashed up things and creatures and then retreated back into their money or their vast carelessness, or whatever it was that kept them together, and let other people clean up the mess they had made." "The Diamond As Big As the Ritz" can have a happy ending for the two lovers because it is a fantasy; but the same plot reappears in *The Great Gatsby*, where for the first time it is surrounded by the real world of the 1920s and for the first time is carried through to what Fitzgerald regarded as its logical conclusion.

There is a time in any true author's career when he suddenly becomes capable of doing his best work. He has found a fable that expresses his central truth and everything falls into place around it, so that his whole experience of life is available for use in his fiction. Something like that happened to Fitzgerald when he invented the story of Jimmy Gatz, otherwise known as Jay Gatsby, and it explains the richness and scope of what is in fact a short novel.

Class Snobbery and Education

Scott Donaldson

Scott Donaldson was for many years the Louisa Colley Professor of English at the College of William and Mary. His books include The Cambridge Companion to Hemingway *(1996) and* Hemingway vs. Fitzgerald *(2001).*

Fitzgerald's experience at Princeton—one of the most prestigious Ivy League colleges in the United States—only deepened his ambivalence toward the upper class to which he felt he belonged. He publicly appeared to be loyal to the school—even tearfully so—throughout his life, according to his daughter, Scottie. But Fitzgerald, ambitious for the highest leadership roles in an institution he regarded as a haven for the upper classes, did not succeed at Princeton. His poor grades froze him out of most extracurricular leadership positions and eventually caused him to be suspended from school. He left Princeton without receiving a degree and maintained a love-hate relationship toward the school for the rest of his life. At the same time that he was courting his alma mater, Fitzgerald was excoriating it in his novel This Side of Paradise. *In* The Great Gatsby, *Fitzgerald expresses his feelings about institutions of higher education in the characters of Tom Buchanan—a former football star at Yale who surrounds himself with friends from the school—and Gatsby himself, who attended an even more prestigious school: Oxford University in England.*

No major American writer is so closely associated with his university as F. Scott Fitzgerald. Partly this is because Fitzgerald sticks in the public consciousness as a sort of perpetual undergraduate: charming, talented, and rather irresponsible. But the association is partly of Fitzgerald's making as well. Princeton bulks large in his first and immensely popular novel, *This Side of Paradise*, and serves as a setting for several stories. Like many another Old Grad, Fitzgerald became more devoted to his undergraduate college the older he grew. He also courted Princeton's approval, ardently and unsuccessfully. . . .

[T]here was no one determining occasion [of his deciding on Princeton] but instead an accumulating impression that Princeton would suit him better than either Yale or Harvard, the only alternatives he seems to have considered.

Of the two, Yale was the more formidable rival—too formidable, for young Fitzgerald's taste. He conceived of Yale men as "brawny and brutal and powerful" (like Tom Buchanan in *The Great Gatsby*) and of Princeton men as "slender and keen and romantic" (like Allenby in *This Side of Paradise* and the Hobey Baker he was modeled on). In a letter Fitzgerald made pen-and-ink sketches of the typical graduate of Princeton (well turned out, Roman in profile), of Yale (an unshaven thug), and of Harvard (an aesthete in monocle and flowing tie). Yet "in preparatory school and up to the middle of sophomore year in college," Fitzgerald wrote in 1927, "it worried me that I wasn't going and hadn't gone to Yale." He regarded Yale as the breeding ground for success. But he wanted "something quieter, mellower and less exigent . . . a moment to breathe deep and ruminate" before plunging "into the clamorous struggle of American life." . . .

In "The Spire and the Gargoyle"—the correct title of the story that eventually appeared in the February 1917 *Nassau Lit*—Fitzgerald attempted to come to grips with the academic troubles that prevented him from taking his place among the leaders of his class. The spire stood for aspiration and high hopes, dashed by the gargoyle, or instructor-preceptor. Matters came to a head in the fall of his junior year when he made up geometry with the aid of tutoring but failed makeup examinations in Latin and chemistry. In November he fell ill with malaria, dropped out of college, and did not return until the following fall. . . .

Fitzgerald did nothing about making up his courses. On a February trip to Princeton he was formally set back into the class of 1918. During the spring he wrote a play for Triangle, but in May it was rejected, and though he once more wrote lyrics for the 1916–17 show and was again pictured as a "showgirl," Fitzgerald was no longer a strong candidate for Triangle president.

Considering his intelligence, Fitzgerald made a remarkably bad academic record. He did so poorly at Newman that he had to pass special entrance examinations before being admitted to Princeton. Once enrolled, he failed three subjects his first semester, took fifth groups (passing, but barely) in three others, and managed but one fourth group—a solid D. In the spring he earned his first 3, or C, and passed everything else except mathematics. For the year he finished in general group 5, on the brink of expulsion. As a consequence, he was declared ineligible to participate in extracurricular affairs in the fall of his sophomore year. Despite that warning, he finished in the fifth general group once again, failing three subjects and taking so many cuts that an extra course was added to his schedule as a penalty. Then came the disastrous fall of 1915, when the roof fell in despite his success at geometry. . . .

John Biggs, who roomed with Fitzgerald on his return in the fall of 1916, once commented that as long as Scott "could devote himself to the English courses, he, of course, did brilliantly." But even there his performance was far from brilliant. Fitzgerald never flunked an English course, but he never made a first group either. . . .

Only in letters did he succumb to what *sounded* like bitterness: "It took them only four months [the fall of his junior year] to take it all away from me—stripped of every office and on probation—the phrase was 'ineligible for extra-curricular activities.'" . . .

Damning and Desiring Social Status

Though he knew that *This Side of Paradise* "rather damns Princeton," Fitzgerald was not prepared for the bitterness of the reaction against his novel. As he wrote years later, "Princeton turned on *This Side of Paradise*—not undergraduate Princeton but the black mass of faculty and alumni. There was a kind but reproachful letter from President Hibben, and a room full of classmates who suddenly turned on me with condemnation." Hibben objected to the impression the book gave "that our young men are merely living for four years in a country club and spending their lives wholly in a spirit of calculation and snobbery." Surely there was more to undergraduate life than mere social striving. As an admissions officer remarked long afterwards, "No one will ever know the damage Scott Fitzgerald did when he called this place a country club." . . .

Which is to say, really, that most of his classmates—many of them products of Eastern prep schools far more prestigious than Newman—were less caught up in the struggle for social dominance than he was. As a reproduction of the Princeton inside Scott Fitzgerald's head, the photograph was accurate enough.

Fitzgerald's college career, like Amory Blaine's, reached its peak during the spring of his sophomore year. He was elected secretary of Triangle, made the *Tiger* board, and on the strength of those credentials was able to choose the eating club of his choice. These clubs marked the pinnacle of social success at Princeton, then and, to a lesser degree, now. Many sophomores spent months in nervous agitation before the annual spring bicker. But few underclassmen understood as thoroughly as Fitzgerald the character of the various clubs and their relative rank on campus.

In his essay on Princeton for *College Humor* (December 1927), he elaborated on the "big four"—Ivy, Cottage, Tiger Inn, Cap and Gown. Four years out of five, he wrote, Ivy was "the most coveted club in Princeton," but occasionally one of the other three mounted a challenge to its supremacy. Cottage was architecturally the most sumptuous, "with a large Southern following particularly in St. Louis and Baltimore." Unlike Ivy and Cottage, Tiger Inn cultivated "a bluff simplicity," placing its emphasis on athletics while maintaining "a sharp exclusiveness of its own." Cap and Gown had begun as an organization of "earnest and somewhat religious young men," but during the last decade "social and political successes have overshadowed its original purpose." . . .

In yet another part of the article, he discussed the social credentials of the college's undergraduates. "A large proportion of such gilded youth as will absorb an education drifts to Princeton. Goulds, Rockefellers, Harrimans, Morgans, Fricks, Firestones, Perkinses, Pynes, McCormicks, Wanamakers, Cudahys and duPonts light there for a season. . . . The names of Pell, Biddle, Van Rensselaer, Stuyvesant, Schuyler and Cooke titillate second generation mammas and papas with a social row to hoe in Philadelphia or New York." The tone of such passages reflects that double vision so characteristic of Fitzgerald. On the one hand he stands back, the amused observer commenting on the barely competent "gilded youth" who like butterflies alight at Princeton "for a season." On the other hand, the very recitation of prominent names suggests that like the mammas in Philadelphia he was subject to titillation through contact with the scions of famous families.

A similar doubleness pervaded his attitude toward the clubs themselves. Though a snowstorm raged outside, it was a glorious March day for Fitzgerald when he turned down bids from Cap and Gown, Quadrangle, and Cannon in order to join Cottage with his old friend from Newman, C.W. (Sap) Donahoe. The following year, he made sure that the results of club elections were relayed to him in his St. Paul exile. Archrival Ivy, he learned, had "signed all they bid except Wilson," who happily went Cottage instead. Yet by the spring of 1917 Fitzgerald was making sport of the whole bicker procedure in a satirical piece for the *Tiger*. This approach may have been encouraged by the anti-club movement of that year, led by Henry Strater among others (in *This Side of Paradise*, Strater appears as "Burne Holiday"). His own idealism "flickered out," Fitzgerald told President Hibben, with the failure of the anti-club movement. But Fitzgerald never lost interest in his own club and its fortunes. Recognizing the superficialities and cruelties of the system, he nonetheless paid a full measure of loyalty to the University Cottage Club.

He maintained this loyalty through times when his relations with Cottage were far from auspicious. In 1920, newly married and newly famous as an author, Fitzgerald managed to get himself suspended from the club. He and Zelda came down from New York to chaperone houseparties the last weekend in April. As chaperones they were far from exemplary: "We were there three days, Zelda and five men in Harvey Firestone's car, and not one of us drew a sober breath." Zelda brought applejack to breakfast in order to convert the eggs into *omelettes flambées*. She wore strong perfume. Scott introduced her as his mistress and was widely believed. He got into brawls and acquired a very black eye. It was, he wrote a friend, "the damnedest party ever held in Princeton."

But he did not anticipate the humiliation that awaited him the following week, when he drove down with Stanley Dell, John Peale Bishop, and Edmund Wilson on May 1 for a banquet of former *Nassau Lit* editors. The men had costumed themselves for the occasion and when Fitzgerald presented himself at Cottage wearing a halo and wings and carrying a lyre, he was ejected from a rear window as a token of his suspension from the club. Drunk or sober, he was deeply hurt. . . .

The Cruelty of the Clubs

In his November 13, 1939 letter to Mrs. [Margaret] Turnbull, he found yet another justification for the clubs. "Nothing would please me better than that the whole snobbish system be abolished. But it is thoroughly entrenched there, as Woodrow Wilson saw." And since it was so strongly entrenched, the only thing to do was to aim for one of the leading clubs. He himself might have felt "more comfortable in Quadrangle" with the literary crowd, but he "was never sorry" about choosing Cottage. As in the larger arena of life, one should try for the best: "College like the home should be an approximation of what we are likely to expect in the world."

In the last analysis, however, Fitzgerald was in favor of the de-emphasis of the club system that eventually came to pass. "I hope," he wrote Ralph Church on December 17, 1940, three days before his death, "that the pictures and membership lists [of the clubs] will be eliminated from *The Bric-a-Brac* proper." Alternatively, the yearbook might "print in addition pictures of all the clubs who eat at tables in Commons." Princeton was slipping behind Harvard and Yale in its attitude "toward this monkey business." What must the non-club men feel when they bring *The Bric-a-Brac* "home with all that emphasis on Prospect Avenue" (where the eating clubs are located)? The Fitzgerald who wrote this letter would have agreed with Edmund Wilson's observation, in 1944, that the Princeton of the teens "gave us too much respect for money and country house social prestige." He might even have seen the wisdom in Wilson's further remark that "Both Scott and John [Bishop] in their respective ways, fell victim to this." . . .

Loyalty and Humiliation

Fitzgerald's mature attitude toward his university resembled that of an ardent suitor. As a young man he had failed at

Princeton: failed to graduate, failed to make the presidency of Triangle, and above all failed to impress his fellows as a man of promise. Consider the votes he received in the "class elections" column of the 1917 *Nassau Herald*.

Most Brilliant	2 votes
Handsomest	2 votes
Prettiest	5 votes
Wittiest	7 votes
Thinks he is (Wittiest)	15 votes
Thinks he is (Biggest Politician)	8 votes
Thinks he is (Best Dressed)	2 votes
Favorite Dramatist (tied with George M. Cohen and 54 votes behind Shakespeare)	6 votes

The image is that of a young man of some wit and attractiveness who seems to think he is rather cleverer than is actually the case. Still more revealing than the actual election results was the way Fitzgerald recalled them. He had been voted first in "the most perfect gentleman category," he later claimed. "I had gone out of my way to be nice to so many people who had nothing and were nobodies and then they rewarded me by this vote." He was ranked second as "best politician," Fitzgerald further disremembered, and (less inaccurately), first in "prettiest," which he regarded less as an honor than a slap. . . .

Fitzgerald himself was tastelessly caricatured in the fall of 1959, when the Princeton band—in the midst of a halftime show at the Yale-Princeton game—played "Roll Out the Barrel" and reeled about in mock tribute to "Princeton's gift to literature, F. Scott Fitzgerald." The incident was especially ill-timed, since Sheilah Graham, who that morning had presented to university president Robert Goheen a sheaf of Fitzgerald manuscripts, happened to be in the stands. The editor of the alumni weekly rose to Fitzgerald's defense: "The mind boggles at the inane spectacle of publicly vilifying the memory of a Princeton alumnus—almost literally dancing on his grave—and especially of one so pathetically devoted to Princeton." In the early 1960s, John Kuehl, then a member of the English department, asked President Goheen to investigate awarding a posthumous degree to Fitzgerald. The suggestion, Goheen reported, met with opposition.

World War I and Class

James H. Meredith

James H. Meredith, a lieutenant colonel in the United States Air Force, is also an emeritus professor of literature at the U.S. Air Force Academy. Meredith edits the journal War, Literature, and the Arts. *His books include* Understanding the Literature of World War I *and* Understanding the Literature of World War II. *He also serves on the board of directors of the Fitzgerald Society.*

In The Great Gatsby, *the connection with World War I is muted but persistent. Fitzgerald perceived bravery, fame—even death in battle—as the highest form of courage. He even endowed these ideas with nobility (although, ironically, as Meredith points out, the greatest American hero to emerge from the war was Sergeant Alvin York, a simple man from the remote mountains of Tennessee). World War I continued to haunt Fitzgerald, chiefly because of its disastrous effects on society. It had left all ranks without moral stability and without the leadership to avoid irresponsibility, indiscretions, recklessness, and corruption. In the novel Gatsby, having survived the war, becomes obsessed with capturing the prewar past: winning Daisy and being accepted by upper-class society. Unlike Hemingway, Fitzgerald, in* The Great Gatsby, *concentrated on the damage the war had done to the world, rather than the damage it had done to himself.*

War is an essential element of F. Scott Fitzgerald's work. While Fitzgerald's fiction, like [Matthew] Arnold's "Dover Beach," is primarily focused on love, war's "confused alarms of struggle" are never far removed. Throughout his adult life, Fitzgerald deeply regretted that he never clashed in combat among "ignorant armies" because like the majority of unwitting young men of his generation, he believed that war was a necessary test of manhood. Of even greater importance to him, heroic death would have been a matter of aristocratic virtue, a recognition that he had achieved the social prominence he always craved.

The Nobility of War

As he did with most issues in his life, Fitzgerald personalized this martial urge to the extreme and imagined that he would die a hero's death. In a November 14, 1917, letter, he writes to his mother about his commission in the U.S. Army and his pending assignment to Fort Leavenworth: "I'll be there three months and would have six additional months training in France before I was ordered with my regiment to the trenches." Fitzgerald, ever the Romantic, seems eager to see action. Yet he is realistic enough to be sensitive to the army's social distinctions: "I am a second [l]ieutenant in the *regular* infantry and *not* a reserve officer—I rank with a West Point graduate." Not satisfied yet in frightening his mother to death, Fitzgerald finishes his letter with this: "If you want to pray, pray for my soul and not that I won[']t get killed—the last doesn't seem to matter particularly and if you are a good Catholic the first ought to. To a profound pessimist about life, being in danger is not depressing. I have never been more cheerful." . . .

Observing Fitzgerald's use of war in his fiction clarifies his multifaceted sensibility and demonstrates that he was a writer of many parts: social historian, Romantic, naturalist, realist, symbolist, allegorist, modernist, and stylist. In general, Fitzgerald's writing about war follows three distinct approaches, representing the trauma of three different conflicts: the American Civil War, World War I, and medieval combat. Fitzgerald used World War I to leverage realism against his instinctual Romanticism and to articulate the tragic role of the

Romantic in the modern world. The American Civil War inspired a brief foray into historical fiction at a low point in his career that led to an interestingly idiosyncratic application of modernist irony to that historic conflict. Finally, medieval allegory allowed him to communicate his vision of the dark future augured by the fascist threat of the 1930s. Thus, war became a method for Fitzgerald to express his inimitable vision of the past, present, and future, particularly concerning how conflict alters society. A wounded patron of the battlefield such as Hemingway might scoff at Fitzgerald's pragmatic use of war, yet stories such as "The Night before Chancellorsville," "The Ice Palace," and "May Day," novels such as *The Great Gatsby* and *Tender Is the Night*, and writing projects such as his 1934–1935 Philippe series reflect a persistent desire to reconcile war with the modern condition. . . .

For his part, Fitzgerald's discovery that the American Dream was only "a dream" took several years of personal nightmares. When he did awake, it was to the reality that the redemptive dream could also be an illusion—even a shared national delusion. Although it would certainly be a further stretch, one could make an argument to include F. Scott Fitzgerald on that Princeton monument as well. Although he died twenty-two years after the Armistice, he was, like [Woodrow] Wilson, also a casualty of a painful peace. Unable to die a hero's death in battle like his literary hero Rupert Brooke, Fitzgerald seemed determined to die a martyr's death in a peace that seemed to have been more disturbing for him than the war had been. In Fitzgerald's life, the fog of alcohol, infidelity, corruption, and depression—the cost of personal indiscretions—proved peacetime corollaries of what [is] called the "fog of war. . . ." In Fitzgerald's case, the fog of moral uncertainty that his generation attributed to the Great War proved a paradoxical influence upon his career, for it was both an inspiration and an impediment to his literary development. . . .

WWI as a Break from the Past

Despite her periodic lapses into mental illness and her propensity for overwrought prose, Zelda clearly understood the symbiosis between World War I and the core of her husband's work. Throughout his career, Fitzgerald never wavered from his view that World War I represented a dramatic break from the past. That break in turn is an essential element in his fiction about the modern world.

While Fitzgerald did not write about combat conditions, he did write about the war's historical effect on the individual, particularly the circumstances of those participants who either were members of the American patrician class or who aspired to be. For example, in "The Rich Boy" (1926), Anson Hunter, the epitome of the social elite, joins the U.S. Navy as an aviator. During training in Pensacola, Florida, he meets both the story's narrator and Paula Legendre, the women he will love throughout his life but never marry. Had it not been for the war, these three people would never have met each other, and the circumstances in the story would have never occurred. . . .

Although Fitzgerald's short fiction conveys World War I as fugitive glimpses of realism, demonstrating his belief that the war was a break from the past, his novels provide a fuller picture. No Fitzgerald novel better conveys the sociological role World War I played in the break from the past than *The Great Gatsby*. . . .

Besides these sociological aspects, the importance of the war in *The Great Gatsby* is conveyed on an individual basis as well. For example, Gatsby first recognizes Nick Carraway as a veteran who, like him, served in the Third Division, Nick as a member of the Ninth Machine-Gun Battalion, Gatsby in the Seventh Infantry. As Nick notes, the war inspires an instant rapport: "We talked for a moment about some wet, grey little villages in France". That these two men talk about the places they both saw establishes their mutual credibility and underscores Fitzgerald's eye for realistic detail and narrative development. It therefore falls to fellow veteran Nick to write this novel about Gatsby the war hero, including a verbatim report of Gatsby's own description of how he "tried very hard to die" in the Argonne Forest. . . .

Gatsby, of course, is a fairly transparent con man, but, strikingly, Nick never seems to doubt this story. Part of the reason may be that such tales of amazing individual heroism were quite commonplace. Gatsby's experiences, in fact, parallel those of the famous Sergeant Alvin York. David D. Lee, in *Sergeant York: An American Hero*, summarizes the hero's much-publicized feats, including at least one interesting detail shared by the fictional Gatsby. . . .

A True Hero

The heroic exploits of York were first made known to the American public in an April 26, 1919, *Saturday Evening Post* article. Fitzgerald was obviously familiar with the soldier's legend—he is mentioned by name in "Dalyrimple Goes Wrong," a 1920 story. The *Post* article on York may have even influenced his depiction of Gatsby as a war hero. At the very least, Fitzgerald would not have had to educate his readers about the plausibility of Gatsby's combat experience. Abundant accounts of battlefield heroics had already done so.

From a military historian's perspective, it is significant that Fitzgerald chose to have his hero fight in the Argonne Forest, for this phase in the larger Meuse-Argonne offensive (September–November 1918) was particularly conducive to the type of small-unit fighting that allowed for heroic feats such as Gatsby's and York's. As Zieger notes, American troops had to replace "mass frontal assaults," which accomplished little more than depleting infantry ranks, with "flanking movements and coordinated small-unit assaults against machine gun nests and heavily fortified German positions." . . .

How do the facts that Gatsby is a bona-fide war hero and Nick a fellow veteran contribute to a reading of the novel?

First of all, they not only make Gatsby a sympathetic character; more important, they make him sympathetic to Nick. This sympathy explains the formation of the strong but otherwise inexplicable bond between these two veterans, which does not exist between them and Tom Buchanan, who seems not to have served in the military during the war at all. Gatsby's desire to win back Daisy may also be motivated by a need to heal his combat traumas: she becomes for him the necessary reward to live for now that he has escaped death in the war. It is an understandable and noteworthy goal considering the horrific experience he has gone through and the lack of anything else he has to strive for. Gatsby's goal of recapturing Daisy's affections after the war separates them thus becomes more existential rather than blindly romantic or naively idealistic. Having faced death in battle, he has to find something to live for in peace. . . .

War's Effect on the Veteran

Although Fitzgerald was interested in the effects of war on the individual psyche, he was also sensitive to its impact on the global stage, at first in America and then later in Europe after he expatriated there in the mid-1920s. By the time that he wrote *Tender Is the Night* a decade later, Fitzgerald had become more interested in portraying how the war affected not just society in the United States but the larger Western culture as well. As Milton R. Stern observes, "World War I changed the human universe, quite literally. The Western world, especially, was never the same again. . . . In its aftermath of enveloping cynicism and profoundly anarchic disillusion, it gave enormous impetus to everything anti-establishmentarian, socially and politically, and to everything existential, personally and culturally". Maybe it was the ambiguous nature of the Armistice or the cynical Treaty of Versailles that laid the foundation for the calamitous peace, but whatever the cause, the effect was still the same: wrenching social change and trauma.

Needless to say, the two decades after the war were a difficult period in which to live, particularly for someone as sensitive to the desire for historical continuity and tradition as Fitzgerald was. . . .

War as a Test of Character

According to Fitzgerald's mistress, Sheilah Graham, the impending Second World War was on Fitzgerald's mind on December 21, 1940, the day of his death. Reading newspaper accounts of the German-Italian pact, he voiced his belief that America would inevitably find itself drawn into the conflict, just as it had two decades earlier. More surprisingly, he announced a desire to travel to Europe to work as a war correspondent as soon as he completed *The Last Tycoon*. "Ernest won't have that field all to himself, then," Graham reports him saying. The image of the dapper author of *This Side of Paradise* hitting the beaches on D-Day or rolling into a newly liberated Paris seems almost absurdly idiosyncratic—but only if one fails to appreciate just how deeply entrenched war was in his thinking. Although there is no way of knowing for sure, the subject may even have come to mind later that afternoon as he read about his alma mater's football team in the *Princeton Alumni Weekly*, his last act before a fatal heart attack claimed him. Princeton, after all, had been home to John Prentiss Poe, that great football hero who died a martyr on a World War I battlefield. Although Fitzgerald's failure to "get over" during that war rendered him—in both his own eyes and those of his contemporaries—somewhat suspect as a commentator on the topic, his fiction is nevertheless saturated with it. Ultimately, his discussions of the matter remind us that wars involve many fronts and that the repercussions at home are every bit as compelling as those experienced in the trenches. Indeed, Fitzgerald's lack of direct exposure to combat may be said to have granted him the distance necessary to assess war from the vantage point of history. While Hemingway, Dos Passos, and others were busy demonstrating the visceral horrors of battle, Fitzgerald sought to understand the way that war defined the character of an epoch, including, most obviously, his own. In this sense, his depictions of its effects on American society and the difficulty of gaining historical understanding in the thick of its upheavals are no less valuable an addition to the literary response to war than works by writers prone to boast of having made it to the frontlines.

Upper- and Middle-Class Waste and Destruction

Kirk Curnutt

Kirk Curnutt is professor of English and department chair at Troy State University in Montgomery, Alabama. His publications include both fiction and scholarship, notably Ernest Hemingway and the Expatriate Modernist Movement *(2000).*

Fitzgerald supported himself with jobs in advertising for ten years after the end of World War I. He earned a reputation for steeping himself in the material culture of 1920s America. Consumerism was a phenomenon mostly associated with the middle and upper classes; they were the ones to whom Fitzgerald's advertising was directed, and they were the ones who gloried in unfettered consumption. Fitzgerald, while he criticized this trend, was also caught up in the culture of consumption: he filled The Great Gatsby *with a reverence for luxury. At the same time, he recognized materialism's capacity for destruction and waste among the monied classes.*

While the Great Boom [of the 1920s] inaugurated an era of prosperity unmatched until the late 1990s bull market, it also inspired criticism for its indifference to intellectual and artistic life. This was a time, after all, when President Calvin Coolidge praised business with a reverence once reserved for religion: "The man who builds a factory builds a temple. The man who works there, worships there". . . .

Business as a Temple

At first glance, Fitzgerald might seem an unlikely ally in the literary critique of 1920s consumer culture, for few writers reveled so blatantly in the "greatest, gaudiest spree in human

Kirk Curnutt, from *A Historical Guide to F. Scott Fitzgerald*. Oxford: Oxford University Press, 2004. Copyright © 2004 by Oxford University Press. Reproduced by permission of Oxford University Press.

history" that was the postwar boom. As early as 1921, Edmund Wilson rebuked his fellow Princetonian for his materialism, which in Wilson's view made him incapable of appreciating the Old World aestheticism that modernists idealized: "You are so saturated with twentieth-century America, bad as well as good—you are so used to hotels, plumbing, drug stores . . . and the commercial prosperity of the country—that you can't appreciate those institutions of France, which are really superior to American ones". This saturation was evident not only in the notorious profligacy with which Fitzgerald conducted his personal affairs; it was prominent, too, in the spend-thrift image he promoted in self-deprecating essays such as "How to Live on $36,000 a Year" and "How to Live on Practically Nothing a Year," both of which appeared in the *Saturday Evening Post* in 1924. Most important, his consumerist fascinations are everywhere evident in his fiction, which luxuriates in the tints and textures of consumable goods. So packed with accoutrements of decor and leisure are many of his descriptive passages that his prose radiates the extravagance of detail that one associates with the catalog copy of high-end retailers. One thinks, for instance, of the famous moment in *The Great Gatsby* when the eponymous hero showers Daisy Buchanan with tailor-made shirts "piled like bricks in stacks a dozen high" in his patent cabinets. . . .

Shirts are but one item upon which Fitzgerald lavishes his prodigious lyricism. Elsewhere, he describes cut-glass bowls, blue porcelain bathtubs, yellow roadsters, chiffon dresses and silk stockings, saffron hats, pink-shaded lamps with blackbirds painted on them, Circassian leather lounges, tortoise-shell eyeglasses (a badge of "slickerhood," according to *This Side of Paradise*), as well of jewels of all varieties, from emeralds to rubies to diamonds—including at least one as big as the Ritz Hotel. . . .

Of course, Jay Gatsby stands as Fitzgerald's richest emblem of the self-deception of pecuniary emulation. As Scott Donaldson has noted, Gatsby's personal style, from his fondness for pink suits, silver shirts, and cream-colored cars to his affected salutations (he calls Nick "old sport"), is so gauche as to mark him nouveau riche: "Given an opportunity, Gatsby consistently errs in the direction of ostentation. His clothes, his car, his house, his parties—all brand him as newly rich, unschooled in the social graces and sense of superiority ingrained not only in [Daisy's philandering husband] Tom Buchanan but in Nick". . . .

Upon meeting Nick . . . Gatsby greets him with a supercilious smile that "understood you just so far as you wanted to be understood, believed in you as you would like to believe in yourself and assured you that it had precisely the impression of you that, at your best, you hoped to convey". Later, while reuniting with Daisy for the first time in five years, Gatsby strikes a nonchalant pose, "reclining against the mantelpiece in a strained counterfeit of perfect ease, even of boredom"—a stance undermined when in his nervousness he knocks a clock off the mantel. Significantly, Nick links his intrigue with Gatsby's transparency to the allure of mass-culture images: "My incredulity was submerged in fascination. . . . It was like skimming hastily through a dozen magazines". Daisy makes the same point shortly before her husband denounces Gatsby as "Mr. Nobody from Nowhere": "You always look so cool. . . . You resemble the advertisement. . . . You know the advertisement of the man—". Noticeably, Gatsby does not respond to this compliment, which to him would not be complimentary at all, for to suggest that his identity is constructed out of commodified images is to impugn the very mechanism of his self-realization. . . .

The main anxiety surrounding female consumerism was willpower, not sincerity. The marketplace may have extended to women the power of choice through its diversity of available colors, patterns, flavors, and aromas, yet it also sought to instill a degree of perpetual dissatisfaction that would encourage their continued spending. . . .

An even more tragic example is Myrtle Wilson, Tom Buchanan's mistress in *The Great Gatsby*. The novel's second chapter details the panoply of consumer items Myrtle gathers around her to convince herself she leads a glamorous and exciting life. In fewer than five pages this lowly mechanic's wife changes clothes three times, switching from crepe de chine to muslin to chiffon. "With the influence of the dress her personality had also undergone a change," Nick reports. "The intense vitality that had been so remarkable in [her husband's] garage was converted into impressive hauteur". This observation substantiates consumer psychologist Paul Nystrom's explanation of why apparel creates such a pronounced effect on the female demeanor: "Change in dress gives the illusion of change in personality. . . . If after completing her work [the housewife] makes a change to an afternoon dress or a street garment, the change makes a lady of her". Yet Fitzgerald questions whether Myrtle is indeed a lady or if she mimics marketplace tastes. From her excessive use of perfume to her fondness for trashy novels and gossip magazines, her interests are not only petit bourgeois but imperiously impulsive: she refuses to ride in a taxi unless it is "lavender-colored with grey upholstery" and hectors Tom into buying a dog for the simple reason that "they're nice to have—a dog". In this way, Myrtle symbolizes the female consumer who derives more pleasure from the accruing of possessions than from the possessions themselves. . . .

Materialism Conquors Nature

The Great Gatsby includes several comparable [reistic] similes and metaphors, most famously Gatsby's comment that Daisy's "voice is full of money". In each case, Fitzgerald dramatizes the modern impossibility of envisioning life through anything but the refracting lens of consumerism. . . .

An American soldier succumbs to a poison gas attack during World War I. Hulton Archive/Getty Images.

Fitzgerald's fiction contains several scenes that convey wonder at the wastage that modern technology made possible in the 1920s. Some cases are relatively minor, as when Nick in *The Great Gatsby* halts his narration to note the "pyramid of pulpless halves" left by the "machine in [Gatsby's] kitchen which could extract the juice of over two hundred oranges in half an hour, if a little button was pressed two hundred times by a butler's thumb". . . .

His most famous image of destruction . . . belongs to the valley of ashes in *Gatsby* that Long Islanders pass on the road into Manhattan. Fitzgerald describes the eerie vista through an ironic agricultural metaphor that suggests the underside of disembodied abundance: this "desolate area" is "a fantastic farm where ashes grow like wheat into ridges and hills and grotesque gardens, where ashes take the forms of houses and chimneys and rising smoke and finally, with a transcendent effort, of men who move dimly and already crumbling through the powdery air". Critics have noted the influence of T.S.

57

Eliot's *The Waste Land* (1922) on this passage. Just as Eliot views the refuse polluting the banks of the Thames as symbolic of humanity's alienation from nature, so, too, Fitzgerald portrays debris as indicative of modernity's capacity to exhaust experience. But while Eliot employs concrete (though fragmented) imagery, Fitzgerald's evocation is more hallucinatory, the "grey land and the spasms of bleak dust which drift over it" imply an almost apocalyptic portent of ecological disaster....

Fitzgerald's depiction of auto wreckage, as with his treatment of disembodied abundance and evaporating values, reflects a tension between moralizing against transgression and indulging in it....

The Meaning of Cars and Driving

The Great Gatsby contains the most extensive depiction of driving as a metaphor for morality. When Nick's sometime girlfriend, Jordan Baker, nearly careens into a group of workmen, she defends herself against the accusation that she is a "rotten driver" by claiming others will compensate for her incautiousness: "It takes two to make an accident".

Yet an earlier wreck at the initial party of Gatsby's that Nick attends impugns the truth of this aphorism. As the evening ends, a drunken guest rips a wheel off his coupé trying to navigate the drive....

The episode foreshadows the tragic moment when Daisy runs over Myrtle after the climactic confrontation between Gatsby and Tom. Here, too, the crowd—including Nick, Tom, and Jordan, who happen upon the accident scene moments after Daisy and Gatsby speed away without stopping—is transfixed by the spectacle. Only this time it is the damage done *by* a car, not *to* it, that captivates. Struck dead in the street, Myrtle becomes an arresting sight, her breast, while not severed like the "amputated" wheel of the coupé, is nevertheless left "swinging loose like a flap". The sight encapsulates the dual appeal that wastage held for Fitzgerald. On the one hand, Myrtle's very public death offers him (through Nick) an opportunity to condemn the immoderation and detachment that causes such accidents: "They were careless people. . . . They smashed up things and creatures and then retreated back into their money or their vast carelessness . . . and let other people clean up the mess". Yet the detailed description of Myrtle's corpse, as with similar scenes in "Automobile Collisions" and other essays on the hazards of driving, invites the reader to gaze in spectatorial awe upon the gruesome damage that technologies such as the automobile wreak. Thus, while Fitzgerald recognizes the moral consequences of wastage, he also acknowledges the captivating allure of wreckage that consumerism encourages.

The Universality of Class Divisions

A.E. Dyson

A.E. Dyson was a professor of English at the University College of North Wales and a reader in English literature at the University of East Anglia. He published many works on a variety of social and literary issues during his lifetime. He retired from teaching in 1982 and died in 2002.

The Great Gatsby *is universally applicable, despite its reputation as the quintessential American novel. This universality derives from the post–World War I imagery Fitzgerald uses. Lower- and working-class men, like George Wilson, live in a chaotic wasteland, and their struggle (which is universal) amounts to little in the end. Similarly, the wealthy, upper-class characters, like the Buchanans, are equally universal in their ability to rely on money and privilege—an advantage that the poor cannot match. Between the two extremes lies Nick Carraway, the middle-class narrator, who can see the foibles of both sides—the plight of the poor and the destructiveness of the rich.*

In 1925 T.S. Eliot found himself as moved and interested by *The Great Gatsby* as he had been by any novel for a very long time. Since then the novel has attracted praise from a great many discriminating critics on both sides of the Atlantic, and the deep interest of first generation readers has been shared by others coming at a later time, and from different backgrounds. My own first reading of *Gatsby* is an experience I still recall vividly, and it has remained for me one of the few novels in any language (*Tender Is the Night* is another) for

A.E. Dyson, "*The Great Gatsby*: Thirty-Six Years After," *Modern Fiction Studies*, vol. 7, no. 1, spring 1961, pp. 37–48.

which the appetite regularly and pleasurably returns. Amazing enough, one reflects each time, that so short a work should contain so much, and its impact remain so fresh. Thirty-six years after its appearance I would say with confidence, then, that *Gatsby* has not only outlived its period and its author, but that it is one of the books that will endure.

Not Just an American Novel

Any new consideration must now, if this is so, be concerned with it as a work which belongs not only to American but to world literature; not only to the immediate soil from which it sprang (prohibition, big business, gangsters, jazz, uprooted-ness, and the rest) but to the tragic predicament of humanity as a whole. This is worth stating at the start, if only because an English critic might otherwise feel diffident about approaching a masterpiece which in many ways is so obviously American, and which has been cited so often in definitions of the peculiarly American experience of the twentieth century. An Englishman will miss, no doubt, many important nuances that to an American will be instantly obvious, and he will be less sure of himself in discussing ways in which Fitzgerald does, or does not, look forward to [J.D.] Salinger, [Saul] Bellow, and other writers of our present Affluent Society. He might, however, hope to see other things (and I am relieved to find Leo Marx lending his support to this hope) which will prove no less important in a final assessment, and which might be *less* easily perceptible at home than abroad. This, at any rate, must be my excuse for venturing, in what follows, to bypass the type of sociological interest usually and rightly displayed, and to consider *Gatsby* as something even bigger than the demythologising of the American Myth. The squalor and splendour of Gatsby's dreams belong, I shall suggest, to the story of humanity itself; as also does the irony, and judgment, of his awakening.

A Waste Land for Poor and Rich

The action takes place in "the waste land" (this phrase is actually used), and is, at one level, the study of a broken society. The "valley of ashes" in which Myrtle and Wilson live symbolizes the human situation in an age of chaos. It is "a certain desolate area of land" in which "ash grey men" swarm dimly, stirring up "an impenetrable cloud, which screens their obscure operations from your sight." This devitalized limbo is presided over by the eyes of Dr. T.J. Eckleburg. . . .

Dr. Eckleburg is an advertisement for spectacles, now faded and irrelevant: put there by some "wild wag of an occulist" who has himself, by this time, either sunk down "into eternal blindness, or forgot them and moved away." As a simple but haunting symbol of the *deus absconditus* [absent God] who might once have set the waste land in motion Dr. Eckleburg recurs at certain crucial moments in the novel. He is the only religious reference, but his sightless gaze precludes the possibility of judging the "ash grey men" against traditional religious norms, and confers upon them the right to pity as well as to scorn. It ensures, too, that though the actual settling of the valley is American, and urban, and working-class (I intend to use the word "class" in this account again, without further apology), the relevance, as in Eliot's own *Waste Land*, is to a universal human plight.

Beneath Dr. Eckleburg's unseeing eyes the ash grey men drift. "Drift" is a word used many times, and with the exception of Gatsby himself, who at least thinks he knows where he is going, it applies to all the main characters, including Carraway, the narrator.

Tom and Daisy, the "moneyed" class, have for years "drifted here and there unrestfully wherever people played polo and were rich together." Tom's restlessness is an arrogant assertiveness seeking to evade in bluster the deep uneasiness of self-knowledge. His hypocrisy and lack of human feeling make him the most unpleasant character in the book, but he is also, when it comes to the point, one of the sanest. In the battle with Gatsby he has the nature of things on his side, so that his victory is as inevitable as it is unadmirable. The discovery that his sanity is even less worthwhile in human terms than Gatsby's self-centred fantasy is not the least of the novel's ironies. . . .

Fitzgerald's ironic awareness of life's perversities is symbolized in the fact that [Myrtle's] one positive quality, her vitality, should find expression in the waste land only as vulgarity and disloyalty, and that it should become the instrument of her death. In the same way, Gatsby's great positive quality—his faith, and the loyalty to Daisy that goes with it—finds expression only as a tawdry self-centredness, and it, too, contributes to his death. . . .

Carraway is the one middle-class character in the novel— vaguely at home in the worlds both of Daisy and of Myrtle, but belonging to neither, and so able to see and judge both very clearly. He is conscious of 'advantages' of moral education that enable him to see through false romanticisms to their underlying insincerity, and savour their bitter ironies. Yet he, too, has his restlessness, as uprooted as everyone else in truth, though more determined than the rest to preserve some "decencies," to cling to some principle of order and sanity in the wreckage.

His family comes from the Middle West. It is proud of having a Duke somewhere in the family tree, but relies in practice for its safety and self-respect on big-business—the "wholesale hardware business" which Carraway never wholly loses sight of as his birthright. He has been made restless by the war, and is now looking for some sort of armour against life in detachment and moral alertness. The "intimate revelations of young men" bore him. He is tolerant of other people, but would escape from the sloughs of emotional despond into some simple pattern of control and acceptance. . . .

A Restless but Stagnant Society

In one sense Gatsby is the apotheosis of his rootless society. His background is cosmopolitan, his past a mystery, his temperament that of an opportunist entirely oblivious to the claims of people or the world outside. His threadbare self-dramatisation, unremitting selfishness, and attempts to make something out of nothing are the same in kind as those of the waste-land society, and different only in intensity. Yet this intensity springs from a quality which he alone has: and this we might call "faith." He really believes in himself and his illusions: and this quality of faith, however grotesque it must seem with such an object, sets him apart from the cynically armoured midgets whom he epitomizes. It makes him bigger than they are, and more vulnerable. It is, also, a quality which commands respect from Carraway: since at the very least, "faith" protects Gatsby from the evasiveness, the conscious hypocrisy of the Toms and Daisies of the world, conferring something of the heroic on what he does; and at the best it might still turn out to be the "way in" to some kind of reality beyond the romantic facade, the romantic alchemy which, despite his cynicism, Carraway still half hopes one day to find. . . .

The tragedy—for it is a tragic novel, though of an unorthodox kind—lies in the fact that Gatsby can go only so far and no further. Faith can still remove sizeable molehills, but is absolutely powerless when it comes to mountains. The ultimate romantic affirmation, "I'll always love you alone" cannot be brought to life: certainly not in the waste land; not when people like Daisy, and Gatsby himself, are involved. Gatsby's faith has to break, in the end, against a reality radically incompatible with it. But in so breaking, it makes him a tragic figure: and unites him symbolically with many men more worthy than himself—with, indeed, the general lot of mankind. . . .

Gatsby has ignored, and disbelieved in, such depressing commonplaces as Carraway's—the depressing commonplaces which are at the heart of Daisy's cynicism, and of the greyness of the ash-grey men. In his own private world past and future can be held captive in the present. His faith allows almost boundless possibilities to be contemplated: and if the "universe" which has "spun itself out in his brain" does happen to be one of "ineffable gaudiness," this does not alter the fact that it is more remarkable, and colourful, than the realities against which it breaks. . . .

He has "broken up like glass against Tom's hard malice": and for this reason he can now be pitied, since Tom's attitude, though conclusively realistic, is also hard, and inhuman, and smaller than Gatsby's own. The reality turns out to be less admirable, less human than the fantasy. The events leading to Gatsby's death symbolize, very powerfully, than his downfall, though inevitable, is by no means an unambiguous triumph of moral powers. His death is brought about by Daisy, who first lets him shield her and then deserts him: by Tom, who directs the demented Wilson to the place where he is to be found; and by Wilson himself—a representative of the ash-grey men who comes to Gatsby, in his disillusionment, as a terrible embodiment of the realities which have killed his dream. . . .

A nightmare of this kind demands some sympathy: and if Dr. Eckleburg is unable to provide it, as he looks down unseeingly upon the drama, then there is all the more call for humanity to supply the need. But Gatsby's "friends" fade away in the hour of death: and Gatsby, whose contribution to his own death has been loyalty to Daisy (the one real and valuable emotion bound up with his fantasy), is left alone at the end. . . .

Solid Values and Aspirations

But not completely alone. His father turns up, with pathetic evidences of Gatsby's youthful aspirations and his generosity as a son; one of the guests who has attended Gatsby's parties attends the funeral; and Carraway himself remains, determined to act in a decently human way. "... it grew upon me that I was responsible, because no-one else was interested— interested, I mean, with that intense personal interest to which everyone has some vague right in the end."

Carraway is also, by now, converted to Gatsby: "I found myself on Gatsby's side, and alone." His final compliment to Gatsby, "They're a rotten crowd. . . . You're worth the whole damn bunch put together" may not add up to much, but it is at least true, and a statement to which everything has been moving. At the very least, it is a recognition that being right about the nature of things is no excuse for being inhuman. In its broader implications, it is part of the larger meaning of the novel: which is that in a tragic and imperfect world scorn and condemnation can often come too easily as attitudes. Human warmth and pity may not be able to set everything to rights: but they are costlier and more decent attitudes than mere judgment; and in the waste land, perhaps juster than judgment itself. . . .

He cannot make reality more acceptable than it is, or find a way out of the waste land, or suggest a cure for the cynicism which is eating out the heart of society. He can, however, prize the highest human values that he sees, and respond to the misfortunes of others with a pity which has in it a feeling for human suffering as a whole. It is characteristic that in the closing sentences he should find in Gatsby's tragic awakening a symbol of the disenchantment of mankind as a whole—and end on a note which, transcending both Gatsby's personal fate, and the *folie-de-grandeur* [folly of grandeur] of the America which he also represents, achieves a universal tragic vision as haunting as any I can think of in a novel.

Two American Dreams in Conflict

Brian M. Barbour

Brian M. Barbour is a professor at Providence College in Rhode Island and has served as editor of The Transcendental Quarterly, *based in Notre Dame. He is the author of* Benjamin Franklin *and* American Transcendentalism: An Anthology of Criticism *(1973).*

Gatsby is sometimes interpreted as a symbolic novel, sometimes as the epitome of realism. These two concepts in the novel are linked not to one single American Dream, but two incompatible dreams. First is the dream of Benjamin Franklin, whose practical philosophy is founded on the fear that tyranny takes away the freedom to control one's own life, and that the way to maintain one's liberty is through economics—money. This is the dream that dominates the class structure in Gatsby. The second, competing dream is Ralph Waldo Emerson's. It stresses inner, spiritual independence and values. Jay Gatsby has progressed to an Emersonian stage in a society that is still Franklinesque.

What I am trying to establish is the kind of representative quality the Buchanans have. For they are not meant to be taken as adequate representatives of the American leisure class ("the rich"); rather they represent a deep and permanent tendency in American life, one that surfaces most spectacularly in the leisure class but which is by no means confined to it. The quality they represent, the tendency they embody, is a moral complacency that finds material wealth both self-validating and its own end. The truth about the Buchanans is that they are blind to any values or standards beyond the ones

Brian M. Barbour, "*The Great Gatsby* and the American Past," *The Southern Review*, vol. ix, January 1973, pp. 288–299. Reproduced by permission of the author.

they enact. It is not that they repudiate any deeper wisdom about life and its ends; it is that they are unaware of any such wisdom. "The curse of ignorance," according to Socrates in the *Symposium,* "is that a man without being good or wise is nevertheless satisfied with himself: he has no desire for that of which he feels no want." It is this curse of ignorance that they embody and moral complacency is the quality they represent. Their debased feelings—their infantilism—have the most serious consequences for human life; but the material wealth which validates the moral complacency also makes thinking about ends and consequences unnecessary. The novel lacks the necessary density and roundedness for the Buchanans to be accepted as anything like adequate representatives of the American leisure class. Read like that the novel is not just brittle but absurd. But they represent a quality, a permanent tendency that runs all through American life and which finds its source in Benjamin Franklin.

The Great Gatsby is about the American dream—so the truism goes. But the truism in this case is too clumsy, for there are actually two American dreams and *The Great Gatsby* is about them both and the way they interact. It is convenient to . . . identify these two dreams with the two figures who first articulated them and thereby brought them to consciousness: Franklin and Ralph Waldo Emerson. . . .

The Franklinian dream . . . is one of self-validating materialism that is ignorant about the inner, positive meaning of the freedom it posits as its end, and is in fact complacently blind with respect to any positive moral values or genuinely spiritual sense of human life. The Buchanans embody it in its least attractive form. . . .

Two Different Views of Self-Reliance

Self-reliance is the foremost Franklinian virtue; it is also the title of Emerson's most powerful essay, and the fundamental differences between the two American dreams can be seen by comparing the inner meanings the concept had for the two men. For Franklin it is a reliance on one's self as an accumulator of wealth. . . .

For Emerson self-reliance was based on trust, but it was decidedly not a trust in the ordinary self of the marketplace. That self had to be redeemed. Self-reliance begins with a reliance on God and it moves through a purgation of the ordinary self. That movement is from the ordinary self existing at the level of Franklinian materialism to the new self that has left materialism behind in order to live in the spirit. . . .

A Means to Rank

Information about Gatsby is scattered piecemeal throughout the novel and accumulates slowly for the very good reason that Nick Carraway has to realize the significance of Gatsby's career and this realization does not come easily. The last piece of the puzzle is provided by the novel's oddest character, Gatsby's father, who does not enter until the last chapter. What he provides pushes the novel to the full limits of its depth and significance. He takes from his pocket a tattered copy of *Hopalong Cassidy* and shows Carraway Gatsby's boyhood schedule scribbled inside the back cover. This schedule associates quite explicitly Gatsby's youthful dreams with the Franklinian version of the American Dream. But Gatsby is not associated with that dream; his is of a different order altogether.

When Gatsby dismisses his servants at the start of Chapter VII he is registering his attitude toward wealth. He cares nothing for it in itself; its only value is as a means to something beyond itself, some fuller, more graceful sense of life of which Daisy is the symbol. Gatsby's is a version of the Emersonian dream: in a great imaginative act he has created himself and set out to explore the possibilities of life. The Franklinian dream was the dream of his youth, but he repudiated that youth and the dream associated with it. Part of his "greatness" lies in his having transcended the limits of the Franklinian world, but it is his fate that this Emersonian greatness will go largely unnoticed in a world whose fundamental postulates are Franklinian. Gatsby's dream matured, but America's did not. . . .

The Franklinian dream leads only to the dead end of money, and the characteristic animus held against the leisure class throughout the novel is associated with their lack of any enlarging vision. The Buchanans possess wealth and its concomitant freedom but they have no idea of living. They just drift "here and there unrestfully wherever people played polo and were rich together". Their concept of life never extends beyond a game. What the novel dramatizes, then, is the conflict between the two American dreams, one whose idea is material wealth and leisure (a restless leisure), the other whose ideal is less restricted and finally spiritual. But the novel argues its point even more closely. The Emersonian dream of the self depends to a certain extent on wealth also, although on wealth as means not as end. The freedom this wealth produces is *freedom-to*, a positive value, one that looks forward to becoming. One way of seeing the conflict is to say that there has been a fundamental confusion of material and spiritual values and that the novel dramatizes this confusion which is deep in American life. The confusion can account for Gatsby's failure—i.e., his unwise location of the meaning of his dream in Daisy.

But Carraway offers another choice. In his final meditation he notes that Gatsby's dream of the future really lies in the past, "somewhere back in that vast obscurity beyond the city, where the dark fields of the republic [roll] on under the night". The transcendental vision collapsed under the weight of the Civil War: that is a primary datum of American intellectual history. Another is that in the vast accumulation of wealth that followed, few noticed that it was gone. Where it endured

([American essayist] John Jay Chapman) or resurges (Martin Luther King) it is a quirk: the American dream is a Franklinian dream. The Emersonian dream is in the possession of the scholars. The older vision was temporarily challenged by Emerson but his dream, which in part was not of this world, ended and the older vision reemerged and changed with the new conditions. It was Horatio Alger, not Emerson, who articulated the sense of the postwar world. . . .

Gatsby embodies the Emersonian dream, perhaps the most attractive quality in American life, and its weakness is his failure. His dream is so beautiful that he assumes that whatever triggers it must also have its haloed quality. The dazzle of the dream leaves his eyes too weak to gaze on ordinary life. Daisy's value for him is purely symbolic; like his shirts or his servants she means nothing in herself. His vision implicitly evaluates American civilization even as it gives dignity and purpose to his life. But while the Franklinian dream is complacently ignorant about the ends of life, the Emersonian dream runs the danger that the dreamer may be transfixed by his end. He may lose his contact with ordinary living.

The Great Gatsby dramatizes the conflict between the two American dreams. It does this because its characters represent fundamental tendencies in American life, and the novel acts its meaning on this representative level. It reveals a profound insight into the American past and the meaning of that past in the present. Fitzgerald dramatizes with a sure touch the moral consequences of the conflict and the moral differences between the two dreams. Moreover, he lays his finger on what is tragically missing in American life: an articulated awareness of moral evil. Both the Franklinian and Emersonian dreams lean too heavily on the thin reed of optimism. What is wanted is the oaken staff of [eighteenth-century American preacher] Jonathan Edwards. The novel, on the literal level, like Gatsby's clothes, always just misses being absurd. But on a different level it reveals, on the part of its author, a rare inwardness with something that one can only call the meaning of American history.

A Corruption of Character

Michael Millgate

Michael Millgate is a Faulkner scholar whose best-known works include The Achievement of William Faulkner *(1966) and* New Essays on "Light in August." *He is an emeritus professor at the University of Toronto.*

Fitzgerald is a social novelist and a critic of class. Other great American social novelists, such as Upton Sinclair, John Steinbeck, Sinclair Lewis, and Theodore Dreiser, concentrate on working- and middle-class characters and on exposing class abuse. Fitzgerald's main characters, on the other hand, are members of the upper classes. Because of this, Fitzgerald may have a greater kinship with English social writers like E.M. Forster, and with Americans like Henry James and Edith Wharton. Gatsby himself, however, was born into the lower class and earned his entry into upper-class society through his illegal businesses. The decline of civilization detailed in the novel is as much an inward loss of character as it is an abuse of social privilege.

Lionel Trilling, in his study of Mr E.M. Forster, develops at some length a comparison between Forster and the American novelist Sherwood Anderson. Even more revealing in certain ways is the comparison to be made between Forster and F. Scott Fitzgerald, and we may usefully set side by side a famous passage from each—the description in *Howards End* of the tide coming into Poole Harbour and the concluding paragraphs of *The Great Gatsby*. Here is Forster: . . .

> England was alive, throbbing through all her estuaries, crying for joy through the mouths of all her gulls, and the

Michael Millgate, "Scott Fitzgerald as Social Novelist: Statement and Technique in 'The Great Gatsby'," *The Modern Language Review*, vol. lvii, July 1962. Reproduced by permission of the author.

north wind, with contrary motion, blew stronger against her rising seas. What did it mean? For what end are her fair complexities, her changes of soil, her sinuous coast? Does she belong to those who have moulded her and made her feared by other lands, or to those who have added nothing to her power, but have somehow seen her, seen the whole island at once, lying as a jewel in a silver sea, sailing as a ship of souls, with all the brave world's fleet accompanying her towards eternity?

And here is the conclusion of *The Great Gatsby*: . . .

And as I sat there brooding on the hold, unknown world, I thought of Gatsby's wonder when he first picked out the green light at the end of Daisy's dock. He had come a long way to this blue lawn, and his dream must have seemed so close that he could hardly fail to grasp it. He did not know that it was already behind him, somewhere back in that vast obscurity beyond the city, where the dark fields of the republic rolled on under the night.

Gatsby believed in the green light, the orgiastic future that year by year recedes before us. It eluded us then, but that's no matter—tomorrow we will run faster, stretch out our arms farther. . . . And one fine morning . . .

So we beat on, boats against the current, borne back ceaselessly into the past.

What is immediately striking is how alike Forster and Fitzgerald are in their imagery, in their use of symbols, in their gift of rhetoric, in their feeling for the native land that lies beneath and beyond the human dramas enacted upon it. In *Howards End* and *The Great Gatsby* they are dealing with the same basic theme, which each sees as a national theme: the conflict between the outer life and the inner life, between, to put it crudely, those who do and those who feel. Forster conducted an intensive exploration of this conflict, which is not for him a clash of black and white, and the movement of the novel is towards resolution and reconciliation. It is difficult for him to make us accept the Wilcox-Schlegel [characters in *Howards End*] marriage—we never do accept it entirely—but at least the difficulty has been directly faced.

If the conclusion of *The Great Gatsby* leaves us with no such feeling of dissatisfaction, that is largely because the movement of the book is circular: the action and the symbolism are designed to illustrate, emphasize and justify Nick Carraway's opening distinction between Gatsby, with his 'heightened sensitivity to the promises of life', and, on the other hand, the 'foul dust [which] floated in the wake of his dreams'. When in the course of Nick's funeral oration—for that is what it amounts to—Gatsby's story is suddenly expanded into a parable of man's fate, the splendour of the rhetoric blinds us to the fact that this is a development for which the action of the novel has not completely prepared us. This may give rise, in retrospect, to certain intellectual doubts about the book. The mode of *The Great Gatsby*, however, is essentially poetic, and on this level the resolution achieved is wholly satisfying.

It is often noted that in *The Great Gatsby* Jay Gatsby's business affairs are revealed only in brief and ambiguous glimpses. . . .

The Spirit of Business

Allusions . . . comprise one important aspect of the confidence trick which Fitzgerald performs so successfully throughout the novel: although we have no idea what the conversation is about we are completely convinced that Gatsby is mixed up in something, and that it is all more or less illegal. And this is sufficient for Fitzgerald's purposes: indeed the very vagueness of Gatsby's background actually enhances his almost mythic stature.

The precise methods by which Gatsby makes his money are irrelevant. What is not irrelevant, however, is the element of illegality involved: this is why Fitzgerald makes such use of an otherwise peripheral character, Meyer Wolfsheim, with his talk of 'business gonnegtions' and his distinction of being, as Gatsby explains, 'the man who fixed the World Series back in 1919'. In stressing the corruption at the heart of Gatsby's dream, as well as exposing, in the revelation of Daisy's character, the tawdriness of what the dream aspires to, Fitzgerald clearly intended a fundamental criticism of the 'American Dream' itself and of the business society to which, in the twentieth century, it had become indissolubly wedded. . . .

The Tricksters

It should now be clear that to speak of Fitzgerald's 'confidence trick' in *The Great Gatsby* is to describe his technique, not to decry it. . . .

The method, as has been suggested, is akin to that of poetry and works primarily through the imagery. Alternatively we might say that it is a cinematic technique, achieving economy, speed and tautness by building up the narrative through the scene rather than the chapter unit, cutting abruptly from one scene to another, using the flashback, creating a total pattern through recurrent phrases, scenes, situations, images. The symbolism of the 'green light' is obvious enough, but scarcely less insistent are such images as Gatsby's yellow car, Daisy's white roadster, the blue lawns of Gatsby's house. We might examine, for the sake of example, the way in which Daisy's representativeness is defined by the images which cluster round her. After the famous moment when Gatsby says that Daisy's voice is 'full of money' Nick, as narrator, goes on:

> That was it. I'd never understood before. It was full of money—that was the inexhaustible charm that rose and fell in it, the jingle of it, the cymbals song of it. . . . High in a white palace the king's daughter, the golden girl. . . .

Prohibition forbid the manufacture or sale of alcohol in the United States during the 1920s, but many Americans wanted it anyway. © Underwood & Underwood/Corbis.

This paragraph is the climax of two strands of imagery which also come together in Daisy's name: the daisy flower is white with a golden centre ('in a white palace . . . the golden girl'). Daisy herself is always associated with whiteness: in chapter I and again in chapter VII Daisy and Jordan Baker sit together on the couch 'like silver idols weighing down their own white dresses', Daisy speaks of their 'white girlhood' to-gether, and Jordan tells Nick that Daisy is a girl 'dressed in white, and had a little white roadster'. This whiteness obvi-ously carries suggestions of innocence, remoteness and inac-cessibility ('the white palace'), but in the first chapter it is al-ready made clear that something more is involved: . . .

The whiteness, that is to say, goes with the life-denying 'absence of all desire' and links up with Nick's final dismissal of Tom and Daisy as 'careless people' who 'smashed up things and creatures and then retreated back into their money or their vast carelessness'. The 'innocence' is destructive, like that of Graham Greene's 'quiet American'; the inaccessibility is a withdrawal from those 'promises of life' to which Gatsby him-self is so sensitive.

The other strand of imagery, culminating in 'the golden girl', is, of course, associated with ideas of wealth. At the be-ginning of the novel Nick speaks of his first actions on com-ing East to live: 'I bought a dozen volumes on banking and credit and investment securities, and they stood on my shelf in red and gold like new money from the mint, promising to unfold the shining secrets that only Midas and Morgan and Maecenas knew.' It is to this sentence that we must refer back the description of the Buchanans' house: outside it is 'red-and-white' and surrounded by roses; inside Daisy and Jordan wait in a room that is 'crimson', 'rosy-colored' and has a 'wine-colored rug' below 'the frosted wedding-cake of the ceiling'. Daisy herself is associated again and again with gold: she has a gold pencil; in Gatsby's bedroom she sees his 'toilet set of pure dull gold' and 'took up the brush with delight, and smoothed her hair'. . . .

Many other examples could be quoted—Gatsby, for in-stance, dresses for his first reunion with Daisy in 'a white flan-nel suit, silver shirt, and gold-colored tie'—but enough has probably been said to indicate the characteristic features of the technique. As so often with Fitzgerald it isn't easy to say just how far was himself aware of what he was doing. . . .

It is a little surprising that Edith Wharton should criticize Fitzgerald for something which he might well have derived from her own method in, say, the presentation of Elmer Moffatt in *The Custom of the Country*. Moffatt's background is very lightly sketched in, but he is seen in action, or on the brink of action, sufficiently, often to convice us, as Christopher Newman probably does not, that he is capable of the achievements attributed to him. This, as we have seen, is exactly Fitzgerald's method in presenting Gatsby, whose history, situation and aspirations are similar to Moffatt's in several important respects. Indeed, it is possible to think of *The Great Gatsby* as representing, in certain ways, a bringing up to date of the American sections of *The Custom of the Country*. Certain important themes occur in both novels: the conflict between West and East within America itself; the relationship between the possession of wealth, social success and 'getting the best girl'; and, above all, the presentation of the money-society of New York, both at its amusements and in its domestic settings, and of the corruption at the heart of that society. . . .

The point is rather that Fitzgerald, as a social novelist, is much closer to Edith Wharton than to any of his predecessors or contemporaries: he works in the same social area, uses similar characters, and views society from much the same standpoint.

A Flawed View of Greatness

Ronald Berman

Ronald Berman is a professor of literature at the University of California, San Diego. A scholar of the English Renaissance and Restoration, his works include The Signet Book of Restoration Drama *(1980). He has also published widely on Fitzgerald, including* Fitzgerald, Hemingway, and the Twenties *(2000).*

Jay Gatsby is the model of a self-invented man. When he first leaves home, Gatsby falls in company with Dan Cody, a man who has successfully created his own identity. But Gatsby soon realizes that Cody's success is not the type that he himself wants. Cody is uncouth—although he has wealth, it does not win him the social position Gatsby craves. Instead, Gatsby turns to magazines and other periodicals: the same media that proclaim the necessity of consumption in establishing class membership.

Jay Gatsby was born Jimmy Gatz around 1890 to shiftless dirt farmers who gave him a past to forget. Thereafter the stages of his life form both a chronology and a reading list. In 1906, in the last flyleaf of a text important to him, "Hopalong Cassidy" (actual date of publication 1910), he enters thoughts about reading and the good life. The self-admonition of going through "one improving book or magazine per week" is connected to "Work," "poise," and being "better to parents". It is a list of rural commandments, designed around not only utilitarian virtues but also a sense of national character. His regimen has led infallibly, his father knows, to "success" and would have resulted in his becoming "a great man" who would "of helped build up the country". That phrase "great man" is important and will be widely intertextual from 1906 to 1922. Greatness is not simply personal; it has public shape and consciousness.

About a year later, approximately 1907, Jimmy Gatz runs away from home and becomes Jay Gatsby. He has lived the life of a roughneck while developing conceptions from somewhere about all the beauty and glamor in the world. But while living with Dan Cody he refuses Dan Cody's life. He is governed by certain standards that make his life Talmudic [the Jewish Holy Book], a series of negative observances that are important for us to grasp. We don't know where he gets his restraint . . . , but it will be important to sense that part of him. Gatsby stays away from what most men pursue, resembling other literary heroes of self-change and discipline. . . . The first measure of his new life is self-control. In that he will be set against other distinctively American heroes who take the road of excess to no particular destination.

Another State of Identity

Having received two kinds of education, he enters another stage of biography and identity. In Louisville, at war, and at Oxford he is accepted as an officer and a gentleman. There is proof positive in 1919: Wolfsheim, who notices these things, recalls that even in trouble Gatsby was "a fine appearing gentlemanly young man". This time, in a complementary way, the emphasis is on externals. They have proceeded from something internal. Manner itself is derived from an idea of restraint that lies behind the idea of being a gentleman.

When Gatsby sums up his own life in 1922 he adds another component derived from many "magazines." Gatsby mentions a number of newsstand themes, among them hunting big game and experiencing epical sadness over lost love. Again, there are the complementary themes of internal sensibility and the mastery of external style. From 1906 to 1922 Gatsby has recreated himself a number of times. Each incarnation not only is a form of fiction but is inspired by fictions for sale. And his "rise," of course, is itself an imitation of a very popular form of fiction on the American scene.

The idea of greatness has, meanwhile, itself undergone a change. The magazines that Nick has recognized (in chapter 4) don't have much to say about actually *working* for greatness. The tactics of day-to-day labor are familiar, but they seem no longer to be interesting. Even Fitzgerald honors the idea of "success" through work more in the breach than in the observance. His heroes depart from the scene, then simply return with their fortunes to tell us where they have been. It might be interesting to learn how money is made in the laundries and drugstores and mines that he mentions—but Fitzgerald's concern does not lie in telling us. . . .

It is important to remain aware that Gatsby's real story is part of democratic mythology. It is rural and proletarian and infused with public ideals. It says a great deal that his life becomes ever more intensely private and that the ideals he begins with, which are prairie American, are replaced by a mythology of a certain style, manner, and status. Fitzgerald has brought the "real" story to textual life, then submerged it under a replacing story that is in many ways its inferior. The two stories have an adversary relationship. They ask us to compare them and to compare our attitudes about them. . . .

What's Good for the Rich Is Good for America

What ideas might a provincial reader have picked up from the mass market of improvement? To judge from Jimmy Gatz, and from Mr. Gatz, personal success was part of national success. To better yourself was to reenact the national experience of economic and hence moral growth. James mentions *The World's Work*, a magazine that relentlessly stated that the creation of wealth was "the product of our national genius"— and a certain proof of our national honor. Mr. Gatz, better informed than he seems to be, knows that we "build up the country" by getting rich. *The World's Work* agrees: "by building up the country" great rich men justify their lives and make *our* lives better. *Collier's* is much more critical of achieved wealth, but the lead editorial of April 29, 1905, mourns those "great figures" who have become rare in America as heroic individualism subsides. Throughout the spring issues of 1905 it recalls the idea of the true businessman-hero whose own success should be a model for that of everyone else....

Gatsby and Protestantism

Fitzgerald wants to believe the liberal Protestant conviction that the self can be remade. In a sense, both Nick and Gatsby have conventional faith in the efficacy of acts, hence in the innocence of motives. God is invisible in this novel not because of the issue of his existence but because human decision determines human fate.... Liberal Protestant hopefulness, with which both Nick's and Gatsby's narratives begin, is displaced by moral realism and the tragic sense of life. Liberal Protestant moral activism, however, had to be retained—as, indeed, it functioned in Fitzgerald's own intensely goal-oriented (and still partly Catholic) life.

As the last pages of *The Great Gatsby* indicate, this language stayed in mind. As I hope to show, the character of "emotional indulgence" in *Gatsby*, especially in Daisy Buchanan, is a surrender to fate in the guise of nervous incapacity. But Nick sees his duty as the formulation of will by restraint with consequent moral action, not as the expression of subjective desire. He knows that desire and will have their imperatives—he respects those romantic imperatives on Gatsby's grand scale—but he is remorseless in his contempt for mere emotional self-interest. Self-interest exhausts the tolerance of a tolerant mind.

The sixth chapter of *The Great Gatsby* takes the liberal Protestant position. Gatsby's dreams proceed from innocence. We don't know quite how material or how sexual they are— the language dims into romantic circumlocution—but they are the work not of the id but the more abstract "imagination." Gatsby, like Nick Carraway, has brakes on his desires and rejects the life of Dan Cody. . . .

The Traditional vs. The New

The sixth chapter debates both nervous energy and restraint of nerves. It tells us that before joining Dan Cody, Gatsby led a sexual life of "overwhelming self-absorption". He does away (without conflict) with the life of the senses. He does not imitate Dan Cody in the pleasures of "an infinite number of women", and he lets liquor alone. It would have been more interesting if *Daisy* had a rival in this story, but given the theory of Gatsby, it would be impossible, even undesirable, for her to have one.

Dan Cody, who is indeed "voluptuous," is part of a group of turn-of-the-century figures in the text. Very little mercy is shown to any of them, because they are historically representative. They are the relics of "the Victorian era" who show in grim satirical detail the fall of its egotism. Fitzgerald has taken a postwar idea and made some modifications. Recent work on the aftermath of World War I by Samuel Hynes emphasizes the presence of a particular kind of villain in writings of the twenties: "Victorian Old Men [who] represented the power of the past over the present . . . [and] the stupidities and the follies of the Victorian past." These figures ruled the pre-war world and oversaw its catastrophe. While public anxiety in the early twenties was often focused on "the younger generation," Fitzgerald had on his mind also that Victorian generation. Some in this group are either ineffectual, like Mr. Carraway, or aware, like Wolfsheim, that their time is over. But there is a much more powerful emphasis: Cody is "physically robust but on the verge of soft-mindedness", while Jordan's aunt brings into the story her twice-defined trait, senility. The self-transcending brewer who built Gatsby's castle is merely daft; Mr. Gatz, worn-out by failure, is at the end of another dismal and even depressing American life.

Cody has been given a rough but useful chronology: he was born about 1857, joined the copper rush after 1875, was sent to sea by his caretaker-mistress in 1902, met Gatsby in 1907, and died hard and mindless in 1912. He is not only of the "real" West but also of the real America, a fact of life irreducible to philosophy. Whatever "civilization" may be, the term used by Tom Buchanan in beginning our social dialogue, and whatever "community" may be, the term used throughout the beginning of the century to identify ideal society, Cody is an impassable barrier to their ideas. He is the real majority; he does what men would do if they could. Fitzgerald has a particular strategy in dealing with wealth here, in "The Rich Boy" and in "The Diamond as Big as the Ritz." He is not concerned with the idea that wealth corrupts: instead, he works with the idea that wealth reveals. It allows personality to display what it *is*, hence its terrifically bad style and solipsism. The possession of wealth means that the possessor does not have to change his desires. Fitzgerald's rich men and women want only to be themselves without interruption. Dan Cody's yacht is simply a movable bar and bed. But we have to sense something about desire—in this text it wants unconsciousness. And it is the strength of both liberal Protestantism and the residual Catholicism of Fitzgerald that they resist this. One might say that it is the work of his novel to show that resistance. . . .

Cody is not simply the sum of life "of the frontier brothel and saloon". His picture is generational, and we learn from him what it means to help "build up the country". He connects to James J. Hill, to Rockefeller, and to Nick's uncle, who exhibits the same hardness of face and mind. If the idea of the frontier is satirically qualified, so is that of the country and its building up. Gatsby, at the beginning of his conscious life, believes that "the rock of the world" is founded on imagination—or, at least, Nick, whose phrase it is, holds this belief for him. But Cody is in the story to state something different, that his world is the real world, both in the novel and in American life. It is occasionally uplifted, and some of its "vitality" spills over into higher things, but it remains unchanged. Most of the characters in the novel agree with him implicitly and imitate him with less success.

The subject of Cody, because of the summary quality, is a useful introduction to the people at Gatsby's second party and especially to Tom Buchanan, who follows hard on the heels of Cody's departure from the text. Tom is Dan Cody in a minor key, disguised by social conscience. His own indifference is hidden in manner and speech. The moment of comedy that attends his meeting with Gatsby is preceded and framed by Cody's open brutality. But the meeting is contrived and slippery with "civilization." It modernizes the Cody episode— there are the same components, men, women, drinks, hospitality. But the mode has become comedy of manners. There is much pumping of hands and twittering of invitations and downing of drinks and earnest worries about social behavior. Above all, there is talk—the scene is all talk and not much consequence. Yet there is one consequence, and this too has its American echoes—there is "lots of room" at the table but not for Gatsby. . . .

We might begin with the judgment . . . by [George] Santayana, defining the great American issue of class responsibility introduced by Tom Buchanan. . .

Tom is a figure in a script he imagines, which goes something like this: he is a descendant of wealth and great social responsibility. He has married rightly and has even educated himself in the mores of his class. He is conscientious, willing to undertake the protection of righteousness. But the role he fulfills goes something like this: although he has lived the life of "pampered incapacity" described by Santayana while dreaming of being one of society's "natural leaders," he defines his responsibility as keeping the "lower orders" down, where they deserve to be. Having become a watchdog instead of a knight on horseback, he brings to a close one drama of genteel idealism, that of the aristocrat with a social conscience. The real script of his life will come into play from this point on. His function will be to exclude, his energies will center on envy, his bravery will be displaced by prudential fear.

Daisy, Jordan, and Myrtle

Rena Sanderson

Rena Sanderson, a professor at Boise State University in Idaho, is the editor of Bowing Bridge: Essays on Hemingway and "For Whom the Bell Tolls" *(1992). She is also a major contributor to the* Cambridge Companion to Ernest Hemingway *and has served as a trustee of the Hemingway Foundation.*

The three principal female figures in The Great Gatsby—*Daisy Buchanan, Jordan Baker, and Myrtle Wilson—all fall into what was, in the 1920s, a new category of womanhood: the flapper. The epitome of the modern 1920s era woman, a flapper was vivacious and liberated, but was also spoiled, rebellious, and self-centered. Fitzgerald is generally given credit for popularizing the literary image of the flapper. At the same time, he let it be known that he had little respect for his creation. In his mind, flappers threatened many positive, traditional values.*

F. Scott Fitzgerald is best known as a chronicler of the 1920s and as the writer who, more than any other, identified, delineated, and popularized the female representative of that era, the flapper. Though it is an overstatement to say that Fitzgerald created the flapper, he did, with considerable assistance from his wife Zelda, offer the public an image of a modern young woman who was spoiled, sexually liberated, self-centered, fun-loving, and magnetic. In Fitzgerald's mind, this young woman represented a new philosophy of romantic individualism, rebellion, and liberation, and his earliest writings enthusiastically present her as an embodiment of these new values. Although she is often seen now as a mere fashion of the bygone Jazz Age, the flapper should be regarded as one of the great authentic characters in American history. . . .

Fitzgerald's Flapper

Fitzgerald's early and widely publicized association with the flapper, however, has led many readers to misconstrue and to oversimplify the author's portraits of women and of relations between the sexes. It is important to understand that, almost from the start, Fitzgerald was ambivalent toward his "creation," fearing that the flapper embodied not freedom but moral anarchy and lack of direction. Increasingly he used her as a symbol not only of a new order, but also of social disorder and conflict. As he wrote to Edmund Wilson in May 1925, "If I had anything to do with creating the manners of the contemporary American girl I certainly made a botch of the job". But the public mistakenly assumed that Fitzgerald, whose early success was tied to the flapper, necessarily endorsed her. In fact, Fitzgerald became the victim of that success. His artistic ambitions were thwarted by the public's desire for more flapper stories, and his association with that one female type prevented readers from appreciating the full range and complexity of his interest in modern women. . . .

While the Gibson Girl [after Charles Dana Gibson, a *Life* magazine illustrator] was shortly supplanted in the public imagination by the more sexualized flapper, who aimed at attracting men, both female types shared a refusal to play the selfless angel whether of the house or of the nation. In fact, they defined themselves by rejecting the established ideal of woman's nurturing, maternal "nature." Noting this shift in moral authority from the family and the community to the individual, some historians have dated the appearance of the flapper not in the 1920s but well before World War I.

F. Scott Fitzgerald was a keen observer of these changes in women's mores and behavior. Throughout many of his earliest stories—read by thousands of women—many golden girls, popular daughters, and debutantes adopt the deportment, fashions, and attitudes of the flapper and sprinkle the magic dust of their high spirits. In spreading these images, Fitzgerald helped to guide women's modernization. In his own stated view, the significance of his early flappers was that they "were not a type—they were a generation. Free spirits evolved thru the war chaos and a final inevitable escape from restraint and inhibitions. . . ."

Turning to Women for Approval

Fitzgerald early came to think of women in terms of social approval and male validation. Biographers agree that Fitzgerald was embarrassed by his mother Mollie McQuillan who represented the moneyed side of the family but lacked social distinction and social grace. Rather dowdy and unkempt in appearance, she was outspoken and enjoyed a reputation as an eccentric. She spoiled her son, but he preferred his father Edward Fitzgerald (a romantic figure of impoverished gentility) and resented it that his mother overshadowed her husband.

Although Fitzgerald in his youth gained valuable mentors and friends—such as Father Sigourney Webster Fay, John Peale Bishop, and Edmund Wilson—he was haunted by his social inferiority and feared rejection. He turned to women for approval. As biographer Scott Donaldson suggests, "If he could win the heart of the girl—especially the golden girl over whom hung an aura of money, beauty, and social position—surely that meant that he had arrived, that he belonged". . . .

Readers familiar with Fitzgerald's earlier fiction will immediately recognize Daisy as Fitzgerald's golden girl and Myrtle Wilson as the lower-class sexualized woman. New in the female cast is Jordan Baker, a champion golfer with a slim, boyish body and "an erect carriage" which she shows off "like a young cadet"—an indication of her androgynous tendencies.

It is through the eyes of Nick Carraway that we get our first glimpse of Daisy and Jordan. Set off by an elegant decor and airy nature images, the two women impress Nick as incarnations of female loveliness associated with a suggestive mix of purity, ethereal weightlessness, adventure, and maybe even

Women dressed in the flapper style do the Charleston, the dance hit of the 1920s, during a contest in 1926. Hulton Archive/Getty Images.

witchcraft: "They were both in white, and their dresses were rippling and fluttering as if they had just been blown back in after a short flight around the house".

From the beginning, however, Nick suspects that the two women are hiding their true selves behind cultivated public fronts. He glimpses in Daisy's sophisticated cynicism a "basic insincerity ... a trick of some sort". The theatrical tendency he questions may reflect the formative influence of popular culture, especially Hollywood, on women's roles....

In "Babylon Revisited" (February 1931), Fitzgerald sought to redeem the image of the young girl by making the girl younger, purer, a symbol of regained honor. But he later explained that this, like his other last [*Saturday Evening*] *Post* stories, "announced pretty much the death" of his young illusions....

It was Fitzgerald's American young girl with her "boyish" characteristics that helped to dismantle established concepts of male and female nature. True, the same Fitzgerald who introduced to the world this spunky young woman in defiance of old codes of morality (and created several delightfully sensitive and unconventional men) mourned the loss of those old codes, the passing of the father's law and the consequent drifting of a feminized, emasculated world. He adhered to old values and did not acknowledge his own androgynous tendencies. Nevertheless, those very tendencies may have been the driving force that sustained his fascination with women, inspired his characterization of exceptional men and women, and allows his work to transcend its own historical contingency. As Ben Jonson said of Shakespeare, and as might be said of all great writers, Fitzgerald was the "Soul of the age" and yet "not of an age, but for all time."

Genteel Women and Flappers

Elizabeth Kaspar Aldrich

Elizabeth Kasper Aldrich is a scholar of gender issues, concentrating on the 1920s and 1930s. She has taught at Yale, the University of Geneva, and the Claremont Graduate School.

There is a seeming contradiction in The Great Gatsby: *on one hand, Fitzgerald seems to be steeped in and an inheritor of the great American Romantic literary tradition, but on the other hand, he presents himself as the signifier of the Jazz Age, which discarded that same tradition. At the center of both approaches is the figure of Fitzgerald's wife, Zelda: the model for Daisy Buchanan and many other female characters in his works. Zelda was an upper-class Southern belle with a long family history of money and influence—characteristics that had attracted Fitzgerald to her in the first place. But she burst out of that tradition and identified herself with the Jazz Age. For Zelda, the upper echelons of society were too limiting to be borne, and she struggled to escape into a new role.*

'They are all Zelda': we say this facetiously, but we might do so in earnest, as Fitzgerald himself did often, in tones ranging from reverent devotion to the most extreme bitterness. What is striking about Fitzgerald's case—and what is particularly challenging to criticism of his work—is how little we seem to be able to avoid saying it one way or the other. The challenge looks at first all negative: to conflate the life and the work is to violate a sacred tenet of the New Criticism to which many of us went to school, to commit that intentional fallacy against which we were so stringently warned. And at its worst, committing the fallacy simply means descending to the kind of gossip which, in this particular case, is and always has been far too common.

Elizabeth Kasper Aldrich, *Scott Fitzgerald: The Promises of Life*. Basingstoke, Hampshire: St. Martin's Press, 1989. Copyright © 1989 by Vision Press. All rights reserved. Reproduced with permission of Palgrave Macmillan, Alkin Books Ltd., and the author.

Wife, Muse, and Model

Yet the very prevalence of such gossip is telling. More than any other American writer who comes to mind, Fitzgerald is associated in criticism as well as biography with a particular, real woman who was at once wife, muse, model and sometimes literary rival. The highly public and well-documented career of his marriage served always as addendum to or even gloss on the work. And as the revelations of Nancy Milford's 1970 biography have made plain, Fitzgerald not only wrote with Zelda as model, he wrote with and from Zelda as *text*: her diaries and letters, essays and short fiction, even medical records relating to her, found their way into his work. Immortality conferred or exploitation committed, Fitzgerald's use of Zelda in his fiction, like his non-literary advertisements of their life together, amounted to an extraordinary kind of collaboration, one which calls for the most careful reconsideration—here is the challenge in its positive sense—of the relationship between text and context and how we interpret it. . . .

If it is a commonplace of Fitzgerald criticism that he had only one story to write, that all of his novels are autobiography, it is equally true that they were first read as a sort of social history. At the time of Fitzgerald's death in 1940 the dominant note of the memoirs and obituary evaluations that appeared was lament at the persistence of that inaccurate and reductive label, 'Chronicler of the Jazz Age'; nevertheless, this was precisely the title and public function which the author courted and profited from at the start of his career. Yet even if we assume that his own life, as he performed and recorded it, could contain and exemplify the *zeitgeist*, the two functions in his writing were not really compatible. For Fitzgerald the self-chronicler was a Romantic of the most lyric stripe, and Fitzgerald the Chronicler of the Jazz Age wanted above all to be a sociologist of the finest accuracy and the weightiest *authority*. . . .

Daisy as Symbol

Daisy 'in life' (the character who lives in the world—both satirically comic and sociologically accurate—of Nick Carraway's narrative) cannot sustain Gatsby's faith in and demands on her as symbol. This is the subject of the work: as it has always been in Fitzgerald, the transmutation or translation of living woman to symbol. In *Gatsby* the translation is of the Daisy whose history and affective life are 'only personal' to the inhuman green light to which Gatsby stretches forth his arms. The difference in this work is that the subject is liberated for once into full clarity and full congruence with its artistic form. Several factors combine to make this possible.

First of all, as several critics have noticed, Fitzgerald is brilliantly served by the split between narrator Nick Carraway and hero (double and profoundly opposite) Gatsby. Not only does this free him from the inconsistencies of one 'cynical idealist' consciousness, it frees him from the Authority (hitherto an area of simultaneous dependence and rebellion) of the woman/subject. Nick is the mildest of cynics, but his world is definitely prose and authoritative ('dishonesty in a woman is a thing you never blame deeply' is one example of the old aphoristic mode). Gatsby is the Romantic idealist, and Fitzgerald had the genius to make him a *bad* poet (hearing Gatsby's version of his life 'was like skimming hastily through a dozen magazines'). When Nick, on the other hand, presents Daisy through Gatsby's perspective—whether he shares or only appreciates it—he rises to lyricism; when at the end he meditates on Gatsby's death, he rises to true poetry.

Second, the role of heroine is split, not into two women characters over whom one man is divided (as in *Tender Is the Night*) but among three women, each of whom is, as it were, assigned to one man. Of course heroine is the wrong term, but we should not discount the extent to which the characters reflect and reflect on each other. Jordan Baker, first presented as indistinguishable from Daisy ('two young women . . . in

95

white') turns out to represent a sort of masculine aspect or alternative: she has, along with name and (sporting) activity, taken on the masculine function of lying about the woman, that is herself. And Myrtle, Tom's vulgar mistress who is presumably beneath illusion or even the right to speak Daisy's name (she is slugged for doing so), nevertheless reveals her twinship in her own flower name, not to mention her sharing of Daisy's husband; she is a heroine in the *poetical rôle* which she, like Gatsby, finally plays: she dies, and in death achieves the dignity at least of surrendering her 'tremendous vitality'. . . .

Finally, Fitzgerald's masterpiece owes much to the unprecedented distance he achieved in it from the immediate realities of his own life. True, he reproduced his myth of his own courtship and seduction of Zelda in Gatsby's of Daisy, but it is here not only relegated to the past but rendered in a manner frankly legendary. The profounder autobiographical truth which he seizes in *Gatsby* comes from what must have been a personal realization, that his survival as a pure Romantic would have depended on his *not* winning his bride. For the irony is that Fitzgerald, that incessant brooder on women and Woman, was not particularly good at rendering full or convincing women characters in his long fictions . . . and only in this work can he transcend—by rendering explicit—his entrapment by one model who must symbolize *all* beauty and illusion—an all which must end as none.

Class and Spiritual Corruption

John W. Bicknell

John W. Bicknell was professor of English at Drew University. His area of specialization was American literature during the 1920s.

Criticism of The Great Gatsby *changed between the 1920s and 1950s, as readers began to realize the importance of class issues in the novel and to see the author's indictment of American society. While many writers and historians see the United States during the 1920s as the apex of social development, Fitzgerald recognized the dark forces that threatened to tear the class system apart. John W. Bicknell, one of the earliest critics to examine the importance of the lower and middle classes in the novel, also elaborates on the callousness of the upper-class Buchanans. He also points out the significance of the waste land—a deliberate echo of T.S. Eliot's famous poem—in which the working-class George and Myrtle Wilson live. But while Fitzgerald understood what was happening in American society, Bicknell concludes, he never embraced the social action that other writers, like John Steinbeck, endorsed.*

One point may be made immediately: we have stopped talking as if Fitzgerald's importance consisted in being a charming Echo of the Jazz Age. We are beginning to see that his evocation of that age carries with it ominous tones of impending disaster. Fitzgerald could hardly complain now as he did to Edmund Wilson that not one of the reviewers of "Gatsby" "had the slightest idea what the book was about."

A Critique of American Class

In 1925 it was perhaps difficult to take seriously a writer who portrayed the beautiful and the rich as essentially damned and

John W. Bicknell, "The Waste Land of F. Scott Fitzgerald," *The Virginia Quarterly Review*, vol. 30, autumn 1954, pp. 67–80. Copyright ©1954 by *The Virginia Quarterly Review*, The University of Virginia. Reproduced by permission of the publisher.

who implied that the American Dream was, after all, little more than a thinly veiled nightmare. In the 1950's we are less likely to misunderstand his intentions. Increasingly, modern critics are recognizing that "The Great Gatsby" is a searching critique of American society. . . .

As we reread "Gatsby" today we are struck by the sharpness with which he seized upon the archetypal theme of the twenties and thirties, and by the fact that he pronounced a sentence of doom over a social order that imagined itself in full flower. For indeed, the atmosphere, the characterizations, and the final violence of "Gatsby" all resound with the chords of moral horror and disillusion. . . .

Central to the novel's total effect, as in [T.S.] Eliot's poem ["Waste Land"], are symbols and images of waste, desolation, and futility. From the outset, the landscape is charged with symbolic overtones. . . .

This is the Valley of Dry Bones, the Waste Land, the dusty replica of modern society, where ash-gray men are crumbling, like Eliot's hollow men. The camera focuses next on the monstrous image of an oculist's billboard—the blue and gigantic eyes of Doctor T.J. Eckleburg, which "look out of no face," but from "a pair of enormous yellow spectacles," and "dimmed a little by many paintless days over sun and rain, brood on over the solemn dumping ground." This grotesque image, reappearing throughout the story, eventually becomes a symbol of what God has become in the modern world, an all-seeing deity—indifferent, faceless, blank. . . .

More effective, perhaps because less self-consciously underlined, are such scenes as the party in Myrtle Wilson's apartment, an image of an action symbolizing hollow lives and empty relationships. In this sordid orgy, the sham camaraderie of whiskey only emphasizes the absence of any really human or humane contacts. . . .

Moreover, a moment's glance at Fitzgerald's characters reminds us that in his vision of society we have only a choice of mindless evils or pathetic follies. Tom Buchanan, the wealthy ex-athlete from Yale, is a liar, a hypocrite, and a bully. The splendor of his surroundings is equaled only by his stupidity and "hard malice." Today we would call him the perfect example of the upper-class Fascist, who, obsessed with fear that the black races may overthrow "Nordic Supremacy," sees himself "on the last barrier of civilization." His fear, however, sharpens his cunning, and his position in society gives him the opportunity to use it. Not only does he lie to Myrtle Wilson, but with ruthless contempt, he exploits her husband, George, as an instrument of revenge on Gatsby. Morally speaking, he is Gatsby's murderer. . . .

The Victims of the Class Divide

The victims—Myrtle and George Wilson, and Jay Gatsby—are not so much vicious as pathetic. Members of the lower middle class, the Wilsons are led to ruin by following ill-conceived dreams of escaping from their dreary lives into the world of glamour. Myrtle, who in her energy resembles Gatsby, seeks escape in an affair with Tom Buchanan. To be "ladylike" she buys a dog; in tawdry finery she queens it over the guests in "her" apartment; but when she tries to assert herself, Tom breaks her nose. Myrtle's last desperate effort to escape ends in violent death, thus mercifully sparing her the knowledge that she was merely Tom's plaything.

Her husband, George, is even more pathetic. He is a sick man, too weak to summon up the energy to provide his life either with significance or with the means of escape. Only in the hysteria incited by the betrayal of his home and the death of his wife does he achieve a moment of intense experience, and what is born in hysteria dies in futile violence. Like many in his position, George is conscious of hostility and frustration, but unaware of the forces pressing on him. Under these circumstances his rebellion proves to be misdirected and self-destructive. Deluded by his obeisance to the rich, George seeks help from Tom Buchanan, his betrayer both in love and in revenge. It is an all too familiar pattern: the rich and powerful maintaining their status by directing middle-class frustrations into fratricidal struggles against scapegoats. . . .

The intensity of Gatsby's dream has, in fact, made him childishly naïve. He is blithely confident that he can regain Daisy and their youthful ecstasy merely by displaying to her his ability for conspicuous waste. To Carraway's warning that "You can't repeat the past," he answers, "Why of course you can." So real has his sentimental vision of Daisy become that he refuses to believe that she has ever cared for Tom, and when in the Plaza suite Tom exposes him for what he is, Jay is unable to detect the revulsion on Daisy's face. . . .

Here then is Fitzgerald's waste land, the "spoiled priest's" brooding lament over the destruction of the American dream, a lament without a benediction and without even a hint of any means by which the waste land may be watered. . . .

For the liberal and radical, a re-reading of Fitzgerald's novels may well strengthen his conviction that contemporary society in its present stage is ruled by a complex of forces destructive of basic human values and subversive of man's vision of the good life. A greater number, however, receiving the same impression, may only be confirmed in their querulous apathy and provided with a further justification for self-pity, and for a passive, though disgruntled, acceptance of things as they are.

Humor in the Service
of Class Criticism

Robert Roulston

Robert Roulston, an emeritus professor of English at Murray State University in Kentucky, is a Fitzgerald scholar and the author of numerous articles on the literature of the 1920s. He is the author of The Winding Road to West Egg *(1995).*

A new understanding of Fitzgerald's treatment of class in The Great Gatsby *emerges by focusing on the centrality of the figure of Tom Buchanan. Buchanan not only strengthens Gatsby's criticism of the upper classes through his arrogance and cruelty, he also serves as an object of ridicule. Buchanan is elevated to stand with the great comic figures of American literature, including Huck Finn's Pap, King, and Duke in Mark Twain's* Adventures of Huckleberry Finn. *He is a dangerous fool, and the ambiguity of Fitzgerald's attitude toward him is indicative of the author's ambivalence toward the upper classes.*

The very rich may or may not be fundamentally different from you and me but, if Tom Buchanan in *The Great Gatsby* accurately reflects the breed, they are certainly funnier. From his grandiose entrance in the first chapter when he descends upon fashionable East Egg with his string of polo ponies to his exit in the final pages when, unrepentant over the damage he has done, he slips into a jewelry shop, Tom is one of the great comic characters in literature. Yet, to read the solemn comments he has evoked, we might think that Fitzgerald had invested him with all the portentous malice of Satan in

Robert Roulston, "Tom Buchanan: Patrician in Motley," *Arizona Quarterly*, vol. 34, summer 1978, pp. 101–111. Copyright © 1978 by the Regents of the University of Arizona. Reproduced by permission of the publisher and the author.

Paradise Lost. Tom has been defined as "the most solid, most damning representative of ante-bellum America," as "corrupt," as a man "without conscience," and even as the "embodiment of evil." . . .

The mark of a comic figure, however, is not how he behaves but how he is rendered. In the Henry IV plays Falstaff [a Shakespearean comic] resorts to armed robbery, accepts bribes, and fills his company with men so physically unfit that they are certain to be slaughtered in battle; Pap Finn [Huck Finn's father in Mark Twain's classic] is a geyser of vicious prejudice and a dangerous man, to boot; the Duke and King [pretending to be royalty in *Huckleberry Finn*] are shameless swindlers who attempt to rob helpless orphans. All act quite as abominably as many a character whose deeds elicit pure terror or rage.

Larger than Life

What these grand comic figures, unlike objects of mere satire, have in common with each other and with Tom Buchanan is a larger-than-life quality. They are not simply made ridiculous so that their creators can expose the follies and failings of a certain group of people. Never mere types, they are imbued with the full power of the author's imagination. And, quite as alive as the hero of any tragedy or of any realistic novel, they inspire not disgust or horror but a laughter that blends compassion with disapproval, comprehension with scorn. Among their most salient features are shrewdness combined with self-evident fatuousness and an exuberant amorality which their own view of life justifies. Thus they substantiate Northrop Frye's contention that "comedy is designed not to condemn evil, but to ridicule a lack of self-knowledge." Such characters have an earthy, even a coarse nature. This nature contributes substantially to differentiating a pure comic invention like Sancho Panza from his master, Don Quixote, who has elements of real heroism and also to differentiating, let us say, Jason Compson (another terrible yet comic figure) in Faulkner's *The Sound and the Fury* from Jason's tragic older brother, Quentin. It also in part distinguishes Tom Buchanan from Jay Gatsby.

Gatsby, with his lies, his poses, his extravagance, and his obsession with the unworthy Daisy Buchanan, is at least as absurd as Tom. But Gatsby's fidelity to his "Platonic conception of himself" and his almost mystical idealization of Daisy give him a spiritual aura and a heroic dimension that virtually preclude laughter as an appropriate response. So too does the lyrical prose in which Fitzgerald envelops him. . . .

Other Plans for Comedy

But, despite Fitzgerald's proclaiming of himself as a disciple of [Joseph] Conrad, his third novel has a non-Conradian degree of humor which ranges from deft satire to near farce. No writer who fancies himself to have composed a *Lord Jim* would contemplate naming his book *Trimalchio in West Egg*. Furthermore most of the other titles Fitzgerald considered before adopting the one he finally used are only slightly less suitable for a tragic work. . . .

But, despite the comic drift of much of *The Great Gatsby*, Fitzgerald was correct in deciding against calling the book *Trimalchio in West Egg*. The comic center, after all, is not . . . Jay Gatsby, but, instead, its patrician, Tom Buchanan, who takes his right to his inherited wealth as much for granted as any noble Roman would have taken for granted the right to his ancestral estate. And so formidable a center is Tom that he often seems on the verge of overwhelming the novel. In fact, Fitzgerald once confessed to Maxwell Perkins: "My first instinct after your letter was to let him [Gatsby] go and have Tom Buchanan dominate the book." Then he added: "I suppose he's the best character I've ever done." Much of the magic Jay Gatsby exerts arises from the sympathy the narrator, Nick Carraway, has for him. But Tom needs no such sympathy nor does he get it. Indeed Nick, who seldom misses an opportunity to disparage Buchanan, informs us that he has a "cruel body", a voice with "paternal contempt in it", a "supercilious manner", a "hard" mouth, and "arrogant" eyes. This is no place to recapitulate the old debate over whether Carraway's judgments are really those of Fitzgerald. Suffice it to say that whether Nick's verbal jabs show a greater hostility to Buchanan than the author possessed, they do not make Tom any less funny than Huck Finn's equally harsh comments about Pap make the latter less laughable. . . .

Tom as Shakespeare's Falstaff

He is also never the least hesitant about braying forth pronouncements on every subject from men's clothing to the impending destruction of the world.

And it is when Tom indulges in the last propensity that he soars to his greatest heights of comic absurdity. There is a comic flaw no less than a tragic one, and the mark of the former is that whenever it asserts itself it punctures all the pretenses of its possessor in an instant. Pap Finn's drunkenness and Falstaff's grossness have their counterparts in Buchanan's irresistible impulse to pontificate on the most inappropriate matters at the most inopportune times, usually in the most fatuous possible language. The fact that his billows of nonsense often bear bits of truth adds another comic twist that we shall examine later. The first such incident occurs in Chapter 1 when, at dinner, Tom, with staggering irrelevance, announces: "Civilization's going to pieces. . . . I've gotten to be a terrible pessimist about things. Have you read 'The Rise of the Colored Empires' by this man Goddard?" And, to Nick's embarrassed negative reply, Tom says: "Well it's a fine book, and everybody ought to read it. The idea is that if we don't look out the white race will be—will be utterly submerged. It's all scientific stuff; it's been proved". Tom's timing and mode of expressing himself are so patently ridiculous that both Daisy and Jordan Baker begin twitting him. But with all the deftness of a bulldozer he continues: "This idea is that we're Nordics. I am, and you are, and you are, and—. . . . And we've produced all the things that go to make civilization—oh, science and art, and all that. Do you see?" . . .

There is, however, a double joke about all these ludicrous incidents. The most obvious one is at the expense of Tom. Here the multimillionaire, ex-football star becomes the unwitting buffoon whose ill-timed, ineptly phrased statements show him to be ignorant, insensitive, credulous, and totally lacking in self-awareness. On this level we get the impression that Fitzgerald was heaping onto this scion of a wealthy Chicago family all that "smouldering hatred of a peasant" he later confessed to having felt toward the leisure class. Also he seems to have been venting upon the former Yale end some of the bitterness Fitzgerald retained throughout his adult life over having failed to make the football team at Princeton. And the fact that Tom possesses some of Fitzgerald's own less attractive qualities makes him seem something of a moral scapegoat for the author. Thus, whereas Nick, Gatsby, and Daisy drink little or nothing throughout the novel, Tom is usually intoxicated or in the process of becoming so. Tom also is guilty of the exhibitionism, self-pity, snobbery, and even downright bigotry of which Fitzgerald at his worst could be capable. Tom's crude boasts about his possessions, his insistence upon monopolizing conversations, and his boorishness are not much different from the bragging that made the young Fitzgerald a virtual pariah for awhile at the St. Paul Academy and at Newman or from the exhibitionism that later drove him to make a fool of himself in Hollywood at a party given by Irving Thalberg when he insisted upon singing a dreadful song before the assembled crowd of professional entertainers. And no doubt Fitzgerald was being a bit harsh when he had Nick refer to Tom's crying over the death of Myrtle Wilson by saying that "he whimpered". Yet Fitzgerald even then must have been aware of his own tendency to wallow in lugubrious emotions—a tendency for which Hemingway would later castigate him so severely. As for snobbery, many of his letters reveal him to have been as vain about his socially prominent ancestors as Tom is of his inherited wealth. . . .

Nick's Insight

Nick, to be sure, comes to realize that all is far from right with the milieu he is describing. But what he notes is not its impending collapse but its loss of romantic possibilities of the kind that have sustained Gatsby for so many years. The great American dream of limitless self-fulfillment appears untenable after what he has seen of the rich and the famous in New York and West Egg. But when he flees at the end to his native Midwest, nothing he says indicates that he is going to huddle there waiting for Armageddon: he merely seems to be retreating into a less sophisticated society.

Buchanan, however, is obsessively aware that the social order is in peril. As we have observed, almost as soon as he enters the pages of the novel he blurts out: "Civilization's going to pieces". Now, the fact that he persists in making this and similarly pessimistic observations throughout the book in a bumbling fashion and that the others ignore or laugh at him accomplishes two things. The manner of delivery makes Tom appear clownish. . . .

Fitzgerald made his wellborn clown the repository of some by no means negligible truths. His world is this world—the world of money, status, real marriages, and real love affairs. And he has as sure an eye for a bogus aristocrat like Gatsby as he has for the phony police dog a street peddler sells Myrtle Wilson. He knows that no *real* Oxford man would wear a pink suit. He also knows how to acquire all the facts about Gatsby as soon as his suspicions about him have been aroused and how to take charge of other people, be they guests at his house or a milling crowd at the scene of an automobile accident.

Of course Fitzgerald preferred Gatsby to Buchanan because he preferred the ideal to the real, the preposterously sublime to the realistically preposterous. But to see Fitzgerald choking in rage over Buchanan's inanities is to do injustice to both his sense of humor and to the hard, clear, practical side of his nature that made him such an acute observer of the scenes around him and such a skilled literary craftsman. Even Nick, who cannot "forgive him or like him," comes to realize that Tom believes his behavior to have been "entirely justified". The Tom Buchanans of this world, like the Falstaffs and the Pap Finns, are like forces of nature. The wise man, knowing them to be as incorrigible as they are perverse, learns to exorcise them with laughter. Railing against them futile.

The Illusion of Class

Tom Burnam

Tom Burnam, a professor at Colorado State University, is best known for his book, Mark Twain and the Machine.

Many critics have interpreted the green light at the end of the Buchanan's dock, which beckons to Gatsby from across the bay, as an example of the impossible upper-class dream that he seeks. But the faded billboard advertising the services of the oculist Dr. Eckleburg is equally symbolic. The billboard has decayed to the point that only Dr. Eckleburg's eyes are still visible, and they gaze constantly over the ash heaps of the wasteland where George and Myrtle Wilson live. The eyes represent a center of stability in the midst of chaos, while Gatsby seeks order in all the wrong places.

There is . . . more in *The Great Gatsby* than a protagonist, a plot, and a green light. Many elements in the story, perhaps, will puzzle the practical-minded, for on the level of simple narrative they cannot be accounted for. What does one make, for example, of the faded blue eyes of Dr. T. J. Eckleburg, those staring, vacant, yet somewhat terrible eyes so much more than an abandoned signboard; of the ash heap and its "ash-grey men, who move dimly and already crumbling through the powdery air" over which the eyes brood changelessly; of George Wilson's despairing mutter as he gazes at the eyes, "You may fool me, but you can't fool God!" . . .

It seems to me a very interesting fact the overt theme of *The Great Gatsby* has little to do, actually, with the novel's use of symbol. It is indeed likely, as a matter of fact, that the subdominant motif—which I hope soon to expose—very often

Tom Burnam, "The Eyes of Dr. Eckleburg: A Re-examination of *The Great Gatsby*," *College English*, vol. 14, October 1952, pp. 8–12. Copyright © 1952 by the National Council of Teachers of English. Reproduced by permission of the publisher.

overshadows what Fitzgerald apparently intended to be his principal theme. Of course, it is true that in making its point about the paradoxical futility of an attempt to recapture the past, *The Great Gatsby* obviously also says much more; one measure of its greatness is the complex and ironic quality of Gatsby's attempt to beat against the current. For he—and he alone, barring Carraway—survives sound and whole in character, uncorrupted by the corruption which surrounded him, which was indeed responsible for him; from his attempt at the childishly impossible he emerges with dignity and maturity. Yet no major work of fiction with which I am acquainted reserves its symbols for the subtheme; the more one thinks about *The Great Gatsby*, the more one comes to believe that F. Scott Fitzgerald may not have entirely realized what he was doing. . . .

But F. Scott Fitzgerald is the one who introduces, I think unconsciously, a fascinating examination of certain values only peripherally related to Gatsby's rise, his dream, and his physical downfall. And, if we turn to this other area, this non-Carraway thematic possibility, we see at once that *The Great Gatsby* is not, like [Joseph Conrad's] *Lord Jim*, a study of illusion and integrity, but of carelessness. Our "second" theme—perhaps the more important regardless of Fitzgerald's original intention—becomes a commentary on the nature and values, or lack of them, of the reckless ones. . . .

Daisy: The Novel's Big Fault

Now, all of this self-analysis, it seems to me, misses the point. The "lack" is there, all right, and Fitzgerald strikes at least a glancing blow when he speaks of the "blankets of excellent prose"—Fitzgerald prose, please note, not Nick Carraway prose; for in the letter to Wilson, Fitzgerald is clearly speaking as author and craftsman. But, still, he misses; for it is doubtful that the "emotional relations" between Gatsby and Daisy *need* any more explaining than they get in the novel. In spite of Peter Quennel's description of Daisy as "delightful," one feels that neither her character nor the quality of her emotional resources justifies any very exhaustive analysis. Certainly one must assume that, if the novel means anything, it cannot concern itself with the love of Jay Gatsby, boy financier, for the pretty wife of Tom Buchanan, football hero. In other words, the point of the Carraway theme, at least, has everything to do with precisely the emptiness of the Gatsby-Daisy "emotional relations"—those same emotional relations which Fitzgerald seemed to feel. I think quite wrongly, it was a "big fault" not to elaborate upon. That Daisy exists both in, and as, an emotional vacuum into which Gatsby, being Gatsby, could attempt to pour only the most obvious and contrived cheap-novel sentimentalism has everything to do with the ironic quality of his final defeat at her hands. And the novel would be the worse, I believe, for the very thing the author says it needs: an exegesis of this vacuum and Gatsby's response to it. Fitzgerald's instinct for craftsmanship, we may be thankful, operated before his analysis as critic.

No, it is not the details of Gatsby's later love for Daisy; nor is it that Gatsby turns into Fitzgerald, though this is closer; nor yet is it (as, says Fitzgerald, Mencken thought) that the central story is "a sort of anecdote"—none of these things is responsible for that feeling of something missing which many readers have experienced but that none seems able to account for. As a matter of fact, what is really "missing" in *The Great Gatsby* is not so much a specific element in plot or even theme; the *sense* of something missing comes, rather, from the inherent confusion of themes, the duality of symbol-structure of which Fitzgerald seems to have been unaware. The book, great as it is, still falls short of its possibilities because its energies are spent in two directions. If *The Great Gatsby* revealed to us only its protagonist, it would be incomparable. Revealing, as it does, perhaps a little too much of the person who created it, it becomes somewhat less sharp, less pointed, more diffused in its effect. . . .

Wealth and Desire

It is commonplace to cite chapter, verse, and semicolon to support the view that Fitzgerald's tragedy was that he had not been born to wealth. . . . Yet to say that Fitzgerald wanted money, and to stop there, seems to me to say nothing. What did he seek that money could, he thought, provide? Or, perhaps more accurately, what did he think the rich possessed, because of their money, that he wanted so badly? . . .

The list which Gatsby's father shows to Nick Carraway is not so important for what the old man thinks it represents, that his son "was bound to get ahead," though this is a part of the Carraway theme. Rather, in its boyish effort to reduce the world to terms in the Chaucerian sense of "boundaries," the "schedule" imposes on the haphazard circumstances of life a purpose and a discipline, just as Fitzgerald the man attempts in his novel the same sort of thing.

Many elements now seem to fall into place. The conversation about carelessness between Jordan Baker and Nick assumes a different stature, and in the thin red circle which Gatsby's blood traces in his swimming pool "like the leg of transit" we can see a meaning: the end-and-beginning within which lies, at least, something else than *khaos*, the mother of all disaster. "It is not what Gatsby was," a student of mine once wrote, "but what had hold of him that was his downfall." "What had hold of him"—and of F. Scott Fitzgerald himself—was the dream that all share who seek to impose some kind of order on a cluttered universe. The meaning Gatsby sought—the "order," if you will—was Daisy; when the betrayal came, his dream disintegrated. . . .

Lionel Trilling thinks that Jay Gatsby "is to be thought of as standing for America itself." Perhaps; everyone is Everyman, in a sense, and Gatsby can stand for America as conveniently as he can stand for himself. But it seems to me that the true significance of *The Great Gatsby* is both more personal and more specific. The "spiritual horror" which Mr. Trilling finds

111

in the novel he ascribes to "the evocation of New York in the heat of summer, the party in the Washington Heights flat, the terrible 'valley of ashes' seen like a corner of the Inferno from the Long Island Railroad ... Gatsby's tremendous, incoherent parties ... the huge, sordid and ever-observant eyes of the oculist's advertising sign." This we may accept; but summer heat and ashes and oculists' signs are horrible not per se but *per causam*. The cause of the horror is, in *The Great Gatsby*, the terrifying contrast between the Buchanans, Jordan Baker, the obscene barflies who descend in formless swarms on Gatsby's house, all symbolized by the gritty disorganized ash heaps with their crumbling men, and the solid ordered structure so paradoxically built on sand (or ashes) which Gatsby's great dream lends to his life. And over it all brood the eyes of Dr. Eckleburg, symbols—of what? Of the eyes of God, as Wilson, whose own world disintegrates with the death of Myrtle, calls them? As a symbol of Gatsby's dream, which like the eyes is pretty shabby after all and scarcely founded on the "hard rocks" Carraway admires? Or—and I think this most likely—do not the eyes in spite of everything they survey, perhaps even because of it, serve both as a focus and an undeviating base, a single point of reference in the midst of monstrous disorder? ...

Here Fitzgerald nearly calls his turn—yet he misses again. For Tom and Daisy retreat "back into their money *or* their vast carelessness." And in the implication of the phrase we see that Fitzgerald was himself unready to give up his old, warm world; that Jay Gatsby was not the only one to pay a high price for living too long with a single dream.

Daisy or Marx?

Ronald J. Gervais

Ronald J. Gervais is a scholar of American literature and a professor of English at San Diego State University.

Fitzgerald, like many intellectuals in the early twentieth century, felt a strong attraction to Communist and socialist ideals. However, his most famous works—including The Great Gatsby—*evoke an intense loyalty to the class system that Marxism said would inevitably be overthrown. Fitzgerald was more interested in Marxism in theory than in practice. After thorough discussion, the author concluded that he could not embrace a political and social theory so at odds with his romantic individualism.*

In major works written during the "Red Scare" just after World War I and during the "Red Decade" of the 1930s, F. Scott Fitzgerald cast his responses to Marxism into the form of ambivalent literary debates in which the opponents express as much attraction for the other side as they do attachment to their own. His biography and correspondence during these periods also reveal his two-mindedness toward leftist ideology. For on this subject, too, Fitzgerald cultivated his famed double vision, his ability, as he describes it, "to hold two opposed ideas in the mind, at the same time, and still retain the ability to function." Fitzgerald uses Marxism as an outlet for his ideals and frustrations; his qualified sympathy for it represents his most extreme protest against the excesses and failings of the *haute bourgeois* class which he describes so charmingly and judges so scathingly, and to which he felt his loyalty

Ronald J. Gervais, "The Socialist and the Silk Stockings: Fitzgerald's Double Allegiance," *Mosaic: A Journal for the Interdisciplinary Study of Literature*, vol. xv, June 1982, pp. 80–91. Copyright © 1982 *Mosaic*. Acknowledgment of previous publication is herewith made.

pledged—even if it seemed to him that the class was historically doomed. He shared what he called a "double allegiance
to the class I am part of, and to the Great Change I believe
in." Unable to reconcile these two loyalties, he developed in
his work an attitude toward Marxism that was neither embrace nor rejection. . . .

Marxism and Class Loyalty

Edmund Wilson asks if it might be possible to hold Marxist
political views and yet "not depict our middle class republic as
a place where no birds sing, no flowers bloom and where the
very air is almost unbreathable." Fitzgerald accomplishes something very close to this. He depicts lovingly the charm and
grace of capitalism's upper classes, yet consistently states his
conviction, born of personal resentment and a sense of historical necessity, that they are doomed. Not entirely enthusias-
tic about this prospect, and with "no faith in the future of my
kind in the supposedly classless society," Fitzgerald creates in
his art a strategy of literary debate that permits him to deal
with his ambivalence.

Fitzgerald's Marxist tendencies are more expressive of capi-
talist culture's disillusion with itself than of hopes for a new
communist order. The appeal of Marxism for him comes not
from any vision of a new social order, different from and beyond bourgeois society, but from a "socialism" that embodies
the highest ideals of bourgeois society. . . .

This idealist reading of Marxism remained consistent with
Fitzgerald over his career. In a letter of 1920, he listed Marx,
along with [Jean-Jacques] Rousseau and [Leo] Tolstoi, as a
man of thought, an impractical man, an "idealist" who has
done "more to decide the food you eat and the things you
think than all the millions of Roosevelts and Rockefellers that
strut for 20 years." And in a late letter to his daughter from
Hollywood, he writes that "poetry is either something that
lives inside you—like music to the musician or Marxism to

the Communist—or else it is nothing, an empty, formalized bore". However materialistic were the ends of Marxism, its origins, as Fitzgerald saw it, were ideal, and not unrelated to bourgeois idealism.

Finally, Fitzgerald could suspend his ambivalences in 1935 only by saying that even though he had been "a Marxist socialist since [he] started thinking," his "writer's instinct" held him back from going all the way.

The separateness of that "writer's instinct" from ideological commitment is made clear in "The Crack-Up" (1936), in which Fitzgerald feels that someone should have helped him to keep his shop open, though "it wasn't Lenin and it wasn't God". And lest any ideologist try to explain too quickly the immolation Fitzgerald sees around him in men of honor and industry, he cautions: "I heard you, but that's too easy—there were Marxians among those men". Fitzgerald decides in the essay to give up his old dream of becoming a Bourgeois Superman, "a sort of combination of J.P. Morgan, Topham Beauclerk and St. Francis of Assisi," and to become "a writer only". Such a concept of the writer as complete individualist and as reduced from total man to the writing function only, immediately drew the fire of John Dos Passos, who in a letter of October 1936 remonstrated with Fitzgerald in the vein of the committed author: "Christ, man, how do you find time in the middle of the general conflagration to worry about all that stuff. . . . We're living in one of the damnedest tragic moments in history—if you want to go to pieces I think it's absolutely o.k.". If cracking up is in question, to the Marxist sympathizer Dos Passos it is the cracking up of a whole world that matters, not of an individual self. Dos Passos could not see that the artist was fulfilling his role by proceeding in Fitzgerald's manner—that is, by looking inward, by exploring his own inner consciousness.

For Fitzgerald, despite his recognition of forces at work in society and the world, it was his own deepest feeling of self

and his hero-worship of other exceptional selves—both lega-
cies from bourgeois individualism—that gave him whatever
sense of orientation he had as a writer. What finally mattered
to him was not the just society but the exalted individual,
though he tried to manage both. . . .

[H]e praised John Reed, the American radical and author
of *Ten Days that Shook the World*, not as a keen observer of
social revolution but as a talented and rebellious young man
of action, such as Fitzgerald himself yearned to be. Despite
whatever radical leanings he professed, Fitzgerald was ultimately less interested in investigating social problems than in
illuminating his own experience and feeling.

Yet part of Fitzgerald did seek a social viewpoint founded
on a practical observation of the facts. He told Malcolm Cowley in 1932, for example, that his "peasant" mother, Molly Mc-
Quillan, was "as realistic as Karl Marx," because she kept telling him, "All this, family is a lot of shit. You have to know
where the money is coming from." But he then proceeds to
tell Cowley how he is descended from Francis Scott Key, to
whom there is a statue in Baltimore. Fitzgerald wonders, at
first jokingly, if they would put up a statue to him, "because
[he] died for communism." But then, more soberly, he imagines a statue to "the author of *The Great Gatsby*!" This mix-
ture of detached social observation and starry-eyed personal
aspiration is Fitzgerald's special gift. It is, Cowley observed, as
if he were describing a big dance to which he had taken the
prettiest girl, and at the same time was wondering how much
the tickets cost and who payed for the music. Fitzgerald knew
as well as any Marxist "where the milk is watered and the
sugar sanded, the rhinestone passed for diamond and the
stucco for stone", but was nevertheless committed to the possibilities of romantic wonder offered by his time and place
and social class. . . .

Romance Above Socialism

Fitzgerald's love for the romantic possibilities of individualism, against any concept of collectivism, puts him ambivalently on the side of the most individualistic of all socioeconomic systems, even when he sees that its freedom has become ruinous. His description of Nicole's shopping trip in *Tender Is the Night* is both an indictment of the moneyed aristocracy and a wonder-song to the glittering life-style open to them. Nicole buys from a great list and buys the things in the windows besides; everything she could not possibly use herself, she buys as a present: beach cushions, love birds, rubber alligator, chamois leather jackets and much more. Then Fitzgerald offers his poetic version of Marxist social analysis, penetrating the veil of appearances to discover the sub-stratum of crude human relations and degradations that private property masks. . . .

Despite its impending doom, the way of life open to the rich is infinitely charming. Its "feverish bloom" and "grace" are insidiously beguiling. . . .

Fitzgerald's own humorous attitude toward Marxism cautions us not to accept his sympathies for it without extreme qualifications. The writer who complains in his *Notebooks* that "in thirty-four and thirty-five the party line crept into everything except the Sears Roebuck catalogue," and who intones with tongue-in-cheek solemnity that, "To bring on the revolution it may be necessary to work inside the communist party," clearly writing from ironic detachment rather than commitment. And if we look at his professions of sympathy throughout his career, we see that they are usually qualified by support for a counterideology which espouses the concept of the superior or autonomous individual. In 1924, for example, he proclaimed himself "a communist." . . . If a proletarian Superman sounds paradoxical, his Jeffersonian communism of 1931 is at least explainable in terms of the Communist Party effort in the 1930s to stress the "revolutionary" and "original democratic" impulses of the Founding Fathers and their documents. In the 1931 interview with a Montgomery, Alabama newspaper, Fitzgerald said he was "a Jeffersonian democrat at heart and somewhat of a Communist in ideals." . . .

Fitzgerald seems to have hoped to the end that individual freedom he knew as a bourgeois artist could somehow be reconciled with the socio-economic critique and concern for justice that he admired in Marxism. If the plight of two friends who had managed their resources wisely, yet had been dragged down in the terrible reverses of 1932 could drive Fitzgerald "more and more toward the red flag about which I have been may-poling at a distance all through the decade," the fact is that he consistently maintained that critical distance. The combination of enthusiasm and skepticism implied in the metaphor is characteristic of his double-vision; he could incorporate Marxism into the moral standpoint from which he examined and condemned his American plutocrats, and yet not be blinded by its ideology from seeing and wondering at their beauty and heroism.

Social Issues in Literature

CHAPTER 3

Contemporary Perspectives on Class Conflict

The Rich Are Different

Richard Conniff

Richard Conniff is a prolific writer on a wide variety of subjects, ranging from natural history to economics. His books include The Energy People: A History of PSE&G *(with James C.G. Conniff);* Irish Walls *(with Allen MacWheeney);* Spineless Wonders, *and* The Ape in the Office.

Fitzgerald once wrote that "The rich are different from you and me." In 2007, with corporate salaries reaching into the hundreds of millions annually while many make less than four dollars an hour, this statement is as true as it was when the author composed it. In the following excerpt from his book The Natural History of the Rich, *Richard Conniff attempts to explore the differences of the rich by applying animal studies to human beings. When members of a certain species (such as apes) acquire more food, they begin to behave differently than others of their kind, and others act differently around them. So do humans, Conniff concludes. In* The Great Gatsby, *we can see this kind of behavior modification in the relationship between the Buchanans and the Wilsons.*

L et's begin with an embarrassing admission. Unlike certain pioneering works in the field of evolutionary psychology, this book did not have its origins on the rock-solid foundation of an attitudinal survey. Nor did it, like many great studies in animal behavior, emerge as a result of ten thousand hours of careful fieldwork watching spiders spin webs. It started with a tip from a stockbroker. I was visiting Monaco on an unlikely assignment for *National Geographic*, and it felt as if I had entered another universe, where even the most casual conversation was liable to veer off at any moment into the surreal. One day, for instance, I was having a friendly drink with two young women seeking starter husbands when one of them asked the other, "Does he still have the Jaguar with the matching dog?" . . .

As a natural history writer, I've always assumed that all individual animals, from the Australian bulldog ant on up to [media executive] Rupert Murdoch, conform, more or less, to the rules of their species. They fit into basic patterns of physiology, territoriality, social hierarchy, reproductive behavior, parental care, and so on, and the ones that don't fit generally get eaten.

So I began to wonder if it wasn't possible to think of the rich in a new light—as animals, that is. . . .

Second, we all hope to be rich ourselves. We are descended almost by definition from people who liked food and sex. From them we have inherited deeply embedded biological drives for status, for waterfront real estate, for landscapes of the English country house variety (derived ultimately from the African savanna), and for a variety of other attractive features often associated with the rich and famous. Moreover, all our disclaimers to the contrary, we long to be like them. We pay attention to the rich as slavishly as a troop of gorillas following the lead of its dominant silverback. We mimic them as aptly as a viceroy butterfly mimics the coloration of a monarch. As in any dominance hierarchy, we also fear the rich. They can use their power to hurt us in ways we hardly recognize. . . .

Moreover, life at the top can be in some ways exceedingly unpleasant. I recently heard a trust fund beneficiary rattle off a list of woes associated with inherited wealth, including social isolation, resentment from peers, rich-bashing from society, betrayal or exploitation by friends, unrealistic expectations from family and society, unequal financial status in marriage, and an absence of all the usual factors (like worrying about the rent) that cause the rest of us to drag ourselves out of bed most mornings in search of bread and a modicum of self-worth. He might also have added that the rich get no sympathy. When you are worth millions of dollars, there is a presumption that you should shut up and bear it. . . .

If men come from Mars and women from Venus, where on earth do rich people come from? Are they, as ordinary people often suspect, an alien life form? Is their blood the color of money? Do they have special antennae, as their press people like to suggest, for picking up distant intimations of profit and loss? Can they see around corners? Is life on Canis Major, the big dog star, really light years apart from the bow-wow world of ordinary runts like you and me? The truth is that rich people are not even a different species from us. They are more like a different subspecies.

The rich themselves often say that they just want to be normal people, leading normal lives. "I just want to be middle class," was a familiar refrain among dazzled Internet millionaires in the late 1990s. Then, to their horror, they got what they wished. This ambivalence about wealth is perhaps sincere, but it's also a little disingenuous. Jeff Bezos of Amazon.com made himself a folk hero of the era as a billionaire who drove a beat-up Honda and celebrated frugality. "I don't think wealth actually changes people," he declared. But at the time he was moving out of his 900-square-foot rental in downtown Seattle to a $10 million waterfront house in the leafy suburb of Medina, where his new neighbors included Microsoft billionaires Bill Gates, Jon Shirley, and Nathan Myhrvold. Then, 7,000 square feet perhaps seeming relatively frugal in this context, he decided to expand the place. Wealth is like that. . . .

A Numbers Game

One afternoon in Aspen, I had coffee with a local craftsman. He was the second person that day to let me know early in the conversation that he didn't need to work for a living. He'd married into a prominent family, and when the name failed to produce a satisfactory response, he said, "They owned General Dynamics," a manufacturer of some of the deadliest weapon systems on Earth. "They owned the Empire State building," he said. "Do you have the *Forbes* 400 list?" he asked. It turned out that they are currently worth about $3 billion. . . .

He was scathing about wannabes. Maybe it was because he was himself a relative newcomer in this world. "You can't pretend to have the speed of a cheetah, when you're really a mule," he said. A new country club in town especially irked him. It created "a different level of Aspen citizen, those who belonged, and those who didn't. It was really terribly exclusive in a way a lot of us resented." He'd signed on as a charter member, just to get in a quick round of golf. But the other members turned out to be, on average, sixty-four years old. Mules, not cheetahs. They needed five-and-a-half hours to complete a round. So having bought his membership at $60,000, he sold out at $175,000 and could savor his righteousness. . . .

Money Doesn't Interest Me

What do they all have in common? Almost all in one form or another expressed the idea that money by itself didn't interest them that much. In the beginning, this sounded like the fourth biggest lie, along with "the check is in the mail," and so on. If so, it was a lie with a great tradition. In the library at The Breakers, their seventy-room cottage in Newport, Rhode Island, for instance, Cornelius and Alice Gwynne Vanderbilt had a white marble mantel bearing the venerable French inscription, "Little do I care for riches, and do not miss them, since only cleverness prevails in the end." Biographer Barbara Goldsmith writes that the Vanderbilts saw no irony in purchasing this mantel, which had been pried off the fireplace of a 400-year-old château in Burgundy. Presumably the builder of the

Billionaire Paul Allen's yacht, the Octopus, *is seen here anchored off Rio de Janiero, Brazil, in 2004. Reported to have cost over $200 million to build, the 126-meter-long yacht is one of the largest in the world.* Vanderlei Almeida/AFP/Getty Images.

château also saw no irony in putting the mantel there in the first place. Rich people have always believed it is their cleverness, their wit, their taste, their athletic ability—anything but their money—that makes them special.

And yet they often acted as if money was the only thing that interested them. They practiced the dull art of price-tag parlor talk: "The trouble with Arnie is that he'll only spend $150,000 for a pilot, when he could get a damned good one for $250,000." They applied price tags with wild, domineering abandon even to the most delicate questions of marriage and family life. A photographer friend who was making portraits of two gorgeous younger wives not long ago overheard one of them discussing a sex act proposed by her aging husband. For better and for worse, the details of this sex act are unknown, except that she refused to participate. So he offered her $100,000 and then $200,000. "I'm not doing it," she said, to which he replied, "$350,000, and that's my final offer." She thought about this for a moment, perhaps contemplating what her mother once told her about the spirit of give-and-take in marriage. Or maybe she was just thinking about the price of a Russian sable fur coat. Then she said, "I'll do it for that." . . .

Pecking Orders

Dominance is an astonishingly new idea in biology, first put forward early in the twentieth century by an obscure Norwegian researcher studying the behavior of chickens. Thorleif Schjelderup-Ebbe coined the term "pecking order" and defined the idea of the dominance hierarchy. For his efforts, he was thoroughly crushed by the Scandinavian biological hierarchy and never gained academic employment. But his ideas caught on. In the 1930s, other researchers coined the term "alpha male" to describe the leader of a wolf pack. Biologists began to see dominance hierarchies almost everywhere.

Unfortunately—and this is the first caveat—they have never come remotely close to agreeing on just what dominance means. Different researchers looking at the same group of animals may identify the dominant individual by any of four common definitions: It's the one who can beat up everybody else but doesn't necessarily need to (the Warren Buffett 800-pound gorilla style of dominance). Or it's the one who displays the most aggression (the school of competition exemplified by Larry Ellison of Oracle, who once quoted Genghis Khan: "It is not sufficient that I succeed; everyone else must fail"). Or it's the one to whom other members of the group pay the most attention (the Richard Branson "Look at me in a wedding dress" paradigm). Or it's the one who gets the first pass at resources like food, sex, or a nice place to sleep (King Fahd of Saudi Arabia has bedrooms reserved for his pleasure in the palaces and yachts of Saudi princes around the world, the equivalent of several dozen $2,500-a-night hotel suites, on call every night, all year long, year after year, though he will almost certainly never visit them).

The obvious problem with these four definitions is that the same animal can easily turn up as the alpha in one study and the beta in another. Researchers who regard control of resources as the defining factor, for instance, tend to believe the dominant individual in a group is *least likely* to display aggression. Everybody else is too scared to challenge his status, except at great intervals. Aggression is more typical, they say, of middle-rank individuals jockeying for position in the hope of an eventual bid for the top. . . .

An Elaborate Code

So how do we read the rest of the unwritten code of social dominance? An alpha wolf establishes his authority by biting a rival on the neck and pinning him to the ground. Rich humans are seldom quite that direct. On the Mexican border one time, I met a beautiful, fast-talking, finger-snapping young woman in spangled earrings and a short skirt. She let me know unabashedly and at every turn the power of her family's money. "I mean, we don't own *everything*," she said. "But we own things that you guys need. That humans need. We own the gas company. We own the industrial park. We own the print shop. We have a construction company. Nobody has anything against us," she said, and then she explained: *"We'll cut off your gas."*

The better class of rich people tend to frown on such crass expressions of power. Well, they frown on them and yearn for them at the same time. People expect Oracle and Microsoft to work out their differences like grownups, in the courtroom, with antitrust lawyers as intermediaries. But how delicious it is when the rivalry surfaces in a personal context. A couple of summers ago, Oracle's stock was soaring and Larry Ellison briefly passed Microsoft cofounder Paul Allen to become the world's second-richest person. Ellison was celebrating aboard his 243-foot yacht off Capri. Then he spotted a 200-foot yacht heading out on a twilight cruise to the village of Positano. It was Paul Allen's *Meduse*, the sort of thing rich people make a point of knowing. When they land the Gulfstream V at Aspen airport, they check out the tail number on the Gulfstream V next door to see how the pecking order stands. So Ellison ordered his captain to crank his yacht's three engines to full speed. He overtook Allen's yacht at forty miles an hour, throwing up a huge wake that sent Allen and his guests staggering. "It was an adolescent prank," Ellison told *The Washington Post* afterward. "I highly recommend it." It was of course also an expression of social dominance. (Foul weather warning: Allen has since moved back up to number three on the *Forbes* 400, while Ellison has fallen behind to number four, and both men now go down to the sea in much bigger ships.)

Twenty-First-Century Flappers

Gloria Goodale

Gloria Goodale is a staff writer of the Christian Science Monitor.

The flappers of The Great Gatsby's *Jazz Age, with all their talentless, coarse but endless publicity, are alive and well in the first decade of the twenty-first century. The most notorious is Paris Hilton, whose chief advantage is being one of the heirs to the multibillion-dollar Hilton fortune. Like Fitzgerald's flappers, Paris enjoys the publicity that her fame and fortune, as well as her behavior, has brought her. Appearing on reality TV, Paris and other young heirs have shown the working class what it is like to be young, famous, and very wealthy. Because of this insight into the lives of the rich and famous, the lower class has developed the habit of being in constant pursuit of wealth. People desire a life of luxury, much like the characters of* The Great Gatsby.

There is a moment in the coming Fox reality show, "The Simple Life," in which hotel heiress Paris Hilton, who has been transported to work on a dairy farm in rural America, asks her host family what a Wal-Mart is. "Do they sell walls there, or something?"

Reality TV Gold

For producers, this is reality-TV gold, because of course, the entertainment value of the show lies in displaying the clueless rich girl as she flaunts her ignorance about the way simple folk live.

The problem with this scenario is that it's not true. Ms. Hilton was tweaking the family—and the producers—for her own fun. "I was joking," she says simply. "I was, like, playing dumb."

As the show unfolds, the girls (Ms. Hilton is joined by her best friend, Nicole Richie [daughter of singer Lionel Richie]), play with our preconceptions about the pampered rich. Perhaps because both the girls and the family turn out to be unexpectedly endearing, the show is delicious fun.

When "The Simple Life" debuts Dec. 2 [2003], it will join two others already on the air—"Born Rich" on HBO, and "Rich Girls" on MTV—that deal with the lives and attitudes of some of our country's most well-known wealthy offspring. Providing entertainment by tweaking the rich is as old as the Greeks. But, say observers, in targeting privileged progeny, these shows actually reveal an important sea change in our attitudes about money and its role in that most basic of American pastimes, the pursuit of happiness.

Making Money Is Most Important

"If you look at studies of what college kids ranked most important back in 1967, contributing to society ranked very high," says Elayne Rapping, media studies professor at State University of New York at Buffalo. "Becoming wealthy was much lower. Today, it's just the opposite."

Several participants in the "Born Rich" film say their parents never mentioned the possibility that their life goals might include anything other than making money.

"[We have] affiliations that don't favor charitable actions," says S.I. Newhouse IV, heir to the *Condé Nast* publishing fortune.

Pursuit of Money Has Become "An Illness"

Many of the young heirs in these various programs, Dr. Rapping points out, were born during the go-go Reagan years, in which greed was considered good in some quarters. They came of age during the stock-market explosion of the 1990s. Today, she adds, "we are living in a world in which the pursuit of money has become what I would dub an illness."

These shows are like giant Rorschach tests, says Paul Schervish, director of the Social Welfare Research Institute in Chestnut Hill, Mass. "The commentaries that we make around the water coolers and living rooms in dealing with the subject of wealth are as much about ourselves as they are about the object of our attention," he says, adding that we look for in others that which we aspire to ourselves.

As we examine the young adults in these various shows, we are taking stock of what Mr. Schervish calls our own moral biographies.

"We are tempted in our views to either adulate or attack the wealthy; to be at their throat or at their feet," he says, primarily because we expect more of them. "We look to the wealthy to have somehow not only greater capacity, but greater character," he says. When they do, we admire them. When they appear to fail on the character front, we feel justified in excoriating them.

Examination of the Wealthy

College student Ivanka Trump [daughter of American business executive Donald Trump] who appears in "Born Rich," knows something about being watched. "As I go into life," she says, "people look at me sometimes in a different way and expect me—or sadly, sometimes want me—to fail in certain ways."

This examination of the wealthy for clues about our own motivations has taken on particular power in today's hyperdeveloped consumer culture.

For the first time in history, observes Schervish, it is possible for middle-class families to taste the kind of life only the rich could afford just a generation ago.

Paris (r) and Nicky Hilton pose for photos at a pre-Oscar event in 2004. AP Images.

"You can buy that Lexus or go on that cruise and be on the same boat with the rich," he says, adding that this shift means more and more choices are no longer dictated by the wallet but by values.

Breeding a Society of Discontent

"Luxuries have become necessities," agrees Diane Wood, executive director of the Center for a New American Dream in Takoma Park, Md. This means that "we are breeding a society of discontent."

While confessing that she herself would not be able to survive without her money (she recently purchased a $1,500 dog carrier for her pet), Hilton herself has a thing or two to say about money and happiness following her experience "roughing it" in middle America.

"I met some people there, and they're so much happier than people I see in L.A., who have so much money. People who didn't have anything were, like, more happy than people I've met out here because it's just all about your family," she says. "And I think it would be a great place to, like, raise kids, instead of raising them in L.A."

The Criminal Class

Gene Mustain and Jerry Capeci

Jerry Capeci and Gene Mustain are specialists in the study of gangsterism. Both are former New York Daily News *reporters. Their books include* Murder Machine *(1992). Capeci is also author of* The Idiot's Guide to the Mafia.

One of the most intriguing characters in The Great Gatsby *is Gatsby's business associate Meyer Wolfsheim, an influential mobster. Fitzgerald suggests that Gatsby's association with Wolfsheim brought him the wealth he spends so freely, and that this wealth was based on smuggling and selling alcohol into the United States during Prohibition (1919–1933). By the middle of the twentieth century, organized crime figures had moved on from smuggling alcohol to infiltrating unions, hijacking trucks, and extorting money from businessmen. John Gotti, who died early in the twenty-first century, was one of the most formidable mob bosses. Gotti and Gatsby share some characteristics in common: they were both reared in poor households, they both aspired to high station, and they both enjoyed lavish lifestyles.*

The day after John Gotti became a grandfather in 1984, he won $55,000 playing "the numbers"—the widely patronized though illegal Family [mafia, or organized crime] lottery. He celebrated by buying his grandson a $10,000 bond, worth $20,000 at maturity.

"Second day of his life, the kid has twenty thousand dollars," John told Dominick Lofaro. "Me, I had two . . . cents."

The Humble Beginnings of a Wealthy Gangster

John Joseph Gotti Jr., born October 27, 1940, in the Bronx, also had a dozen brothers and sisters. He was the fifth child of

Gene Mustain and Jerry Capeci, from *Mob Star: The Story of John Gotti*. New York: Penguin, 1988. Copyright © 2002 by Gene Mustain and Jerry Capeci. Used by permission of Alpha Books, an imprint of Penguin Group (USA) Inc.

a construction worker and his wife, Fannie. Two brothers and twin sisters, all less than 5 years old, preceded him. And over the next 11 years they were joined by four more boys and two girls. Two other siblings died during childhood.

John Joseph Gotti Sr. was a hard-working but low-earning man of Neapolitan origin. With 13 kids in 16 years, he was barely able to provide. When the namesake son's freedom was at stake in Brooklyn more than four decades later, his lawyer painted a portrait of a proud man whose fastidious appearance lay in the fact that he overcame a childhood of severe deprivation.

"He doesn't apologize for growing up poor," Bruce Cutler would say. . . .

The same forces that affected Italian Harlem caused John's family to move away from the Bronx during the middle of his fourth year at P.S. [public school] 113. They moved into a two-story wood-frame house on East Thirteenth Street in Sheepshead Bay, a tranquil community in the far southeastern corner of Brooklyn, near the Atlantic Ocean.

John enrolled in P.S. 209; classmates included kids whose parents had achieved more prosperity than the Gotti clan. John began to see that in some minds a kid's status was unfairly tied to his parents' status, which was measured by income. It wasn't his fault he was poor; a little river of resentment began to flow through John, and occasionally it bubbled up as a cocky strut and a sharp tongue. . . .

Teens at Franklin K. Lane High School had many competing street gangs to choose from. John joined the Fulton-Rockaway Boys. Brother Peter already was a member; brothers Richard and Gene signed up later. Another member was Angelo Ruggiero, a pudgy-faced, pigeon-toed kid who was called "Quack Quack" and became John's pal. As was the custom, the Fulton-Rockaway Boys, whose name came from a street intersection a few blocks from school, adopted special colors; theirs were black and purple, the color of bruises. In such gangs, poor teenagers found self-esteem and group identity. The year John joined the Fulton-Rockaway Boys, Marlon Brando starred as Johnny, the rebel hero of *The Wild One*, a popular film about a gang taking over a town. . . .

Youth Gangs of New York

In 1952, the future crime boss completed the sixth grade. This was the year 12-year-old Johnny Gotti, according to Bruce Cutler's trial portrait, went off "on his own"—and the year the Gotti clan was forced to move again after their house was sold.

John's parents had few housing options. They finally moved to the Brownsville-East New York area of Brooklyn, a neglected working-class community that was home to thousands of southern Italian immigrants and Eastern European Jews who had abandoned stacked Manhattan ghettos. . . .

The Rockaway Boys also feuded with the Ridgewood Saints, a particularly violent gang, according to Matthew Traynor, an ex-Saints gang leader who went on to bank robbery and other crimes. In one fight, a Rockaway bled to death after he was stabbed and tossed through a window. Another incident involving a Rockaway landed Traynor in jail. . . .

Eventually, the neighborhood's older gang members, who called their gang a Family, heard about this boy who talked like a politician and wasn't afraid. Pivotally, two of these adult-gang members were Carmine and Daniel Fatico, who, the boy-gang members knew, were connected to a large Family led by Albert Anastasia, who was so important his name was only whispered.

The Fatico brothers operated out of a storefront they called The Club and were active in hijacking, extortion, gambling, and loan-sharking. They killed only when necessary, the boys thought. Carmine was older and cagey; he had been pinched more than a dozen times but had hardly spent any time in jail.

New York City mob boss John Gotti appears in court. AP/Wide World Photos.

Besides the Fatico brothers, plenty more of the wrong role models lived close by. Two of them, Wilfred "Willie Boy" Johnson and William Battista, would become important members of John's crew in Ozone Park. Willie Boy was a sausage stuffer by day, a bookmaker by night, a part-time boxer, and part American Indian. He had a violent and justifiably tough reputation, having fatally stabbed his brother-in-law and survived a bullet to the head fired by the dead man's friend.

Battista was a gambler, too, but his early fame was based on a truck hijacking he had staged using inside information from a secretary who lived on Bergen Street, around the corner from John. Battista waited until the truck driver took his coffee break at the time and place the girl indicated, and then just hot-wired the rig and drove off with $75,000 worth of new clothes. . . .

En route to the majors, John made rookie mistakes. At 17, he was arrested for burglary after he and a few confederates were caught in the act of stealing copper from a construction firm. He pleaded guilty and was placed on probation.

The terms of his probation required him to shun unsavory places and characters—a nearly impossible burden for anyone in Brownsville-East New York. Now a committed juvenile delinquent, John continued to hang out in poolrooms, bars, bookie joints, and racetracks.

In 1959, he was arrested for the first time as an adult. The charge was unlawful assembly; he had been caught in a raid on a gambling location. Theoretically, he had violated his probation and could have been jailed immediately. Instead, he was allowed to remain free. Nearly a year later, after he had been arrested again and fined $200 for disorderly conduct, the unlawful assembly charge came up on the court calendar. . . .

The Adult Gangster Class

He wasn't making much money, however. Between the family and the car and the hanging out, he was always broke. And he and [wife] Victoria kept having kids: three in three years. Angela was followed by another girl, Victoria, and a son, who was named John. Money woes and his nocturnal touring of pool halls, gambling dens, and honky-tonks caused the young parents to fight; they separated several times.

Some separations were forced. In 1963, John went behind bars for the first time—20 days in a city jail after he and Salvatore Ruggiero, Angelo's brother, were arrested in a car reported stolen from the Avis rent-a-car company. Salvatore was a bright boy who would go far in crime, too, but not as a Family man. Sal would become a very rich drug dealer. . . .

He was acquitted of the January charges, but pleaded guilty to the attempted theft and was jailed for several months in 1966. This cost him his job with the Barnes Express Company and a lot of goodwill with his wife. Struggling to support three small children whose father was a jailbird caused her to seek public relief from the New York City Department of Welfare and to file support petitions against him in Domestic Relations Court in Brooklyn.

Any reluctance to completely embrace crime as a way of life melted away in the wake of these humiliations. In the next year, John would not find another job; he would become a professional hijacker.

John was only 26, not too old to seek the education or training which might have opened a legitimate door of opportunity. But he was too impatient and too scornful. He had a wife, three kids, and expensive appetites. He had them *now*. What could he be? A store manager? An insurance salesman? *Forget about it.*

When John thought of successful men, he thought of Carmine and Daniel Fatico. They wore fine clothes and drove big cars. At the track, they could lose with cheer as opposed to despair. They were respected, maybe not by the wider world, but by the young men of John's world.

The Club and Class

Mike Morris

Mike Morris, editor-in-chief of The DePauw, *the oldest student newspaper in Indiana, broke the story of the Delta Zeta scandal a week before the* New York Times *and other national newspapers picked it up. Morris went on to win a prize for in-depth reporting from the Granville, Ohio,* Sentinel.

F. Scott Fitzgerald recognized the importance of what a later generation would call "networking" in The Great Gatsby. *The influence of a fine college and the reputation of its clubs and fraternities were well known in the 1920s, and the exclusiveness of these social organizations was felt to be crucial to one's social status in adult life. It was commonplace for members of fraternities, sororities, and other social organizations to remain close for the rest of their lives, and to help each other in advancing their careers. These facts stayed with Fitzgerald throughout his career.*

Class consciousness in fraternal organizations remains an issue at the beginning of the twenty-first century. In 2007, the Delta Zeta sorority at DePauw University expelled twenty-three members, giving as its reason that the women did not meet standards of attractiveness. Some of the expelled members later indicated that they felt they were also targeted because of their ethnicities.

Twenty-three members of Delta Zeta sorority—half of the chapter—were asked in early December to leave the house in a move national organizers say will strengthen the house by its centennial at DePauw in 2009. Six others have since chosen to leave.

Trouble started last August, when junior Sarah Carlson, a former officer, said national representatives gave the officers

Mike Morris, "DZ 'Reorganizes,' Loses 29 Women," *The DePauw*, vol. 155, February 2, 2007, pp. 1, 3. Reproduced by permission.

two options: improve recruitment or choose not to participate in rush. Too small a pledge class or a vote not to participate in rush would result in the closing of the house.

The officers brought the matter before their sisters, and after one deadlocked vote, the women chose not to participate in rush.

Carlson, who was asked to leave, attributed the vote to a sense of disillusionment with recruitment.

"We were just tired of fighting all year," Carlson said. "We were tired of trying to fight the system. . . . We just wanted to enjoy the year together."

But everything changed Sept. 12, when two Delta Zeta national representatives met with Greek Life Director Tom Hansen and Dean of Students Cynthia Babington. Closing the chapter, Hansen said, would not guarantee Delta Zeta a place on campus when it came time to reopen—their proposal to start a new chapter would be one of many.

The sorority's national Executive Director Cindy Menges was surprised by the news.

Complex Politic of the Greek System

"Wow, OK," she said. "What do we do now?"

Of the alternatives Hansen presented to Menges and the sorority's national Vice President Kathi Heatherly, the two chose to conduct a membership review to identify the women willing to commit to recruitment.

For years, DZ has been DePauw's smallest sorority. Menges said the chapter's struggle with recruitment was caused by the perception of the chapter as being unsuccessful.

"Delta Zeta was the odd man out because we just didn't have as many numbers as the other groups," she said.

Senior Morgan Murphy, who is one of six women staying in the chapter, sees overcoming these perceptions as the task awaiting those women who remain.

"I've seen a lot of girls go through Delta Zeta's recruitment process and seem like they're having a great time . . . and everybody thinks they're going to go there, but when it comes right down to it, they won't go there," she said. "And it's not because of the women, it's because of the stigma of being a Delta Zeta. . . . We're trying to move beyond the stigma."

Two consultants from headquarters are now living in the house and have spearheaded a marketing push to distinguish the Delta Zeta of last semester from the house they're attempting to build. The effort has included the posting of flyers around campus and the delivery of letters and even desserts to other greek chapters.

One of the consultants, Liz Urso, said the chapter has participated in formal recruitment this week but is focusing on a more informational approach.

The move, termed a "reorganization," sent a ripple through the campus community.

"I do not think it's fair to disrupt a chapter and the lives of women who thought they were going to live in that house for a year to tell them in the middle of the year they have to move," said University President Robert G. Bottoms in a mid-December interview. "I also do not think matters were handled in a very sensitive manner. Even if you're justified in taking the actions that they took, why in the world would you do it the week before finals?"

Communication Breakdown

DZ women said things first got fuzzy at the Sept. 12 meeting. They said the national representatives told them things—particularly about the membership review conducted in mid-November—that would turn out to be false. Uncomfortable with the situation, four women took alumnae status even before the review began.

Menges said Delta Zeta as a national organization does not typically conduct member reviews.

"We're not saying that we're free of mistakes," Menges said, admitting the process could have been clearer.

Sophomore Lindsey Kinker, who was asked to leave, remembers being told that women uncomfortable with the plan could take alumnae status voluntarily. Carlson and sophomore Joanna Kieschnick, who was invited to stay but chose to leave, recalled Heatherly saying similar things.

Heatherly said even if she can't recall her exact words Sept. 12, she knows her intentions were good.

"What they thought we meant wasn't what we meant, and we're sorry for that," Heatherly said. "We're certainly willing to say that we're sorry."

At the same time, Heatherly said, the women may have "heard what they wanted to hear" at the meeting.

Menges said if the women recommended for alumnae status had fought to remain in the sorority, they could have circumvented the recommendation. No one has done so, she said.

During the membership review, however, Kieschnick and Carlson each recalled asking their interviewer whether they could remain active members if they were recommended for alumnae status.

"We were told that if we were recommended for alumnae status we would have no say in the matter," Carlson said. "If we tried to challenge it they would deactivate us."

Kieschnick said she received the same response.

Party More but Losing Out

Junior Rachel Pappas, the chapter's former secretary, took unofficial notes at the Sept. 12 meeting. Her notes showed Heatherly suggesting the women bend the rules and perhaps party more.

"I am a . . . national vice president, and if you think that I'm going to go out to a chapter and tell them to bend our national rules and risk my 25 years of service in Delta Zeta . . . then I'm sorry, but I would not do that," Heatherly said, but added: "There is a social climate to the DePauw greek community . . . I'm not talking about drinking, I'm talking about socializing and getting out and meeting people and making friends."

To Carlson, the whole process seemed wrong. She said she thought things had been finalized when the women voted not to participate in rush Aug. 20.

"We thought that we had made the decision for them, and they couldn't change what we decided," she said.

The Aftermath

Each woman interviewed received a letter Dec. 2 informing them of nationals' decision.

There are competing theories as to why some women were asked to stay and others to leave. Senior Cindy Geiger, who was asked to stay but chose to leave, said she thought it was social networks: if the interviewers liked someone, they'd identify her closest friends and invite them to stay.

Menges said the choices were based solely on the member's ability to commit to recruitment.

"During that membership review, if someone tells you that they love Delta Zeta . . . but I really don't have the time you're asking me for, we said that's part of what our problem is, ladies. We've got to have the commitment," Menges said.

Kinker said her life is less stressful without the time commitment of greek life, but that she was willing to help the plan succeed.

"I told them it was hard for me to live in a house on this campus, but I was willing to do whatever it was to participate and be a part of this organization," she said.

Geiger said she knew even before opening her letter she wouldn't stay.

"I just didn't like the idea that they could ask active, dedicated members who did nothing wrong . . . to leave their own chapter," she said.

Sisterhood Not Enough

Ultimately, the process has embittered women on all sides. As it stands, the women who accepted alumnae status were paid $300 to cover the difference between room and board at DZ and University housing. Most have moved into Bloomington Street Hall or North Quad.

But the business-like attitude of this process did not appeal to Geiger.

"I wish that nationals could have found a way to market what we had with the sisterhood and market that to make it appealing," she said.

Making matters worse, senior Crystal Drummond said a few days after she received the letter asking her to take alumnae status she received another letter asking her to donate money to the Delta Zeta Foundation. She declined.

Murphy took a broader view.

"Greek life is about image and popularity and numbers and those are all areas where Delta Zeta lacked, despite the fact that we had amazing sisterhood," she said. "Obviously, on DePauw's campus, sisterhood alone isn't enough to keep a sorority alive."

For Further Discussion

1. Identify two of the writers included in this volume who hold different views of Gatsby. Evaluate their positions.

2. Drawing on the articles and your own reading of *The Great Gatsby*, examine Fitzgerald's feelings toward the upper class in the novel and compare them to those of today's society. (See Bewley, Millgate, and Morris.)

3. Write a paper on the portrait of the lower class in the novel. Is it negative or sympathetic? (See Bewley.)

4. Examine Gatsby's character. Is he primarily sympathetic or unsympathetic? Does he ever see the upper classes for what they are? (See Cowley, Meredith, Curnutt, and Dyson.)

5. Describe Fitzgerald's portraits of upper-, middle-, and lower-class women. Compare them with the current views of the early twenty-first century. (See Sanderson and Goodale.)

6. Examine Fitzgerald's social view of class. Is he a traditionalist or a leftist? (See Millgate, Burnam, Gervais, and Conniff.)

For Further Reading

Theodore Dreiser   *An American Tragedy.* New York: Boni and Liverright, 1925.

F. Scott Fitzgerald   *The Beautiful and the Damned.* New York: C. Scribner's Sons, 1922.

F. Scott Fitzgerald   *Flappers and Philosophers.* New York: C. Scribner's Sons, 1920.

F. Scott Fitzgerald   *Tender Is the Night.* New York: C. Scribner's Sons, 1934.

F. Scott Fitzgerald   *This Side of Paradise.* New York: C. Scribner's Sons, 1920.

William Dean Howells   *The Rise of Silas Lapham.* Boston: Ticknor, 1885.

Henry James   *The American.* London: Ward Lock and Co., 1877.

Henry James   *The Wings of the Dove.* New York: C. Scribner's Sons, 1902.

Sinclair Lewis   *Babbitt.* New York: Harcourt Brace and Co., 1922.

Edith Wharton   *The Age of Innocence.* New York: D. Appleton and Co., 1920.

Bibliography

Books

Frederick Lewis Allen	*Only Yesterday: An Informal History of the 1920s.* New York: Harper and Row, 1931.
Herbert Asbury	*The Great Illusion: An Informal History of Prohibition.* New York: Doubleday, 1950.
Matthew Bruccoli	*Profile of F. Scott Fitzgerald.* Columbus, OH: Charles E. Merrill, 1971.
Kenneth F. Eble	*Scott Fitzgerald.* New York: Twayne, 1977.
William Fahey	*F. Scott Fitzgerald and the American Dream.* New York: Crowell, 1973.
Frederick J. Hoffman. Ed.	*"The Great Gatsby": A Study.* New York: Charles Scribner's, 1962.
Alfred Kazin. Ed.	*F. Scott Fitzgerald: The Man and His Work.* New York: Collier Books, 1967.
Christopher Lasch	*The Revolt of the Elites.* New York: W.W. Norton, 1995.
Page Smith	*Redeeming the Time: A People's History of the 1920s and the New Deal.* New York: McGraw-Hill, 1987.
Brian Way	*F. Scott Fitzgerald and the Art of Social Fiction.* London: St Martin's Press, 1980.

Periodicals

E.C. Bufkin — "A Pattern of Parallels and Doubles: The Function of Myrtle in *The Great Gatsby*." *Modern Fiction Studies*. Vol. 15 (winter 1969–1970): 517–524.

Jeffrey Louis Decker — "Gatsby's Pristine Dream: The Diminishment of the Self-Made Man in the Tribal Twenties." *Novel*. Vol. 28 (fall 1994): 52–71.

Barbara Ehrenreich — "The Rich Are Making the Poor Poorer." Alternet. http://www.alternet.org/workplace/53962/. June 13, 2007.

Martin Kallich — "F. Scott Fitzgerald: Money and Morals." *University of Kansas City Review*. Vol. 15 (summer 1949): 271–280.

Kenneth S. Knodt — "The Gathering Darkness: A Study of the Effects of Technology in *The Great Gatsby*." *Fitzgerald/Hemingway Annual*. Vol. 8 (1976): 130–138.

Alberta Lena — "Deceitful Traces of Power: An Analysis of the Decadence of Tom Buchanan in *The Great Gatsby*." *Canadian Review of American Studies*. Vol. 28 (1998): 19–41.

Michael Millgate — "Scott Fitzgerald as Social Novelist." *English Studies*. Vol. 43 (February 1962): 29–34.

Kermit W. Moyer — "*The Great Gatsby*: Fitzgerald's Meditation on American History." *Fitzgerald/Hemingway Annual*. Vol. 4 (1972): 43–57.

Robert Ornstein — "Scott Fitzgerald's Fable of East and West." *College English*. Vol. 18 (December 1956): 139–143.

Alan Reynolds — "Class Struggle?" The Cato Institute. May 19, 2005.

Joseph N. Riddel — "F. Scott Fitzgerald, the Jamesian Inheritance, and the Morality of Fiction," *Modern Fiction Studies*. Vol. II (Winter 1965–1966): 331–350.

Michael Santoli — "Rich America, Poor America." *Smart Money*. January 23, 2007.

Gary Scharnhorst — "Scribbling Upward: Fitzgerald's Debt to Horatio Alger, Jr." *Fitzgerald/ Hemingway Annual*. Vol. 10 (1978).

Silicon Valley Blogger — "Does Achieving Wealth Make You 'Upper Class'? Facts about Class." *The Digerati Life*. July 12, 2007.

Jim Webb — "Class Struggle: American Workers Have a Chance to Be Heard." *Opinion Journal*. November 15, 2006.

Index

A

American Dream, 25–29, 47, 61, 67–72

   See also Victorian era

American upper class

   animal behavior studies applied to, 120–127

   as careless, 35, 59

   characteristics of, 23–24

   college social organizations and, 39–43, 139–144

   common traits of, 123–127

   as cynical and hypocritical, 64–65

   education and, 39, 40, 42

   greed and, 129–132

   as an illusion, 108–112

   irresponsibility and, 58

   money as sole value of, 120–127

   "networking" and, 139–144

   nouveau riche v., 54–55

   social clubs and, 139–144

   as spiritually corrupt, 97–100

   as wasteful, 53–56

   World War I effect on, 45–52

Androgyny, 92

B

"Babylon Revisited" (Fitzgerald), 91

Baker, Jordan, 58, 90–91, 95–96

Biggs, John, 38

Buchanan, Daisy

   as based on Zelda Sayre Fitzgerald, 93, 94, 96

   as deceptive, 90–91

   as emotionally shallow, 109–110

   imagery portraying, 54, 56, 76–78, 90–91

   as representing American tendency, 67–68, 70

   as romantic symbol, 69, 95–96

Buchanan, Tom, 50, 67–68, 70, 86–87, 101–107

C

Carelessness, 108–112

Carraway, Nick

   middle-class identity and qualities of, 60, 63

   narrator role of, 19, 66

   as reflecting dichotomy of American dreams, 70–71

   as social commentator, 103–104, 106

   wartime experience of, 48–49

Cody, Dan, 80, 81, 84–86

Conrad, Joseph, 103, 109

Consumerism, 54–56, 58–59, 128–132, 129–130, *131*

Coolidge, Calvin, 53

"The Crack-Up" (Fitzgerald), 115

Criminal class, 133–138

Crowley, Malcolm, 116

The Custom of the Country (Wharton), 79

D

Delta Zeta scandal, 139–144

Destruction, 56–58

"The Diamond as Big as the Ritz" (Fitzgerald), 35

Donaldson, Scott, 54–55, 90

Dos Passos, John, 51–52, 115

E

Eckleburg, T.J., 62, 65, 98, 108, 112

Eliot, T.S., 57–58, 60, 62, 97

Emerson, Ralph Waldo, 68–72

F

Fitzgerald, Edward, 17

Fitzgerald, F. Scott, 20, 27

  ambivalence of, 36–44, 95–96, 113–118

  American social class structure in work of, 23, 24–35

  consumerism and, 54

  double vision of, 113–114

  education of, 36–38

  family background and youth of, 17

  Forster comparison with, 73–75

  impact of World War I on, 51–52

  literary influences on writings of, 19

  Marxism and, 113–118

  materialism of, 54

  money's role in works of, 24–25

  overview of, 16

  Princeton years of, 36–39

  as romantic individualist, 116–118

  as social novelist and class critic, 73–79

  social struggles of, 39–41, 43

  as sociologist, 94

  Wharton comparison, 79

  World War I impact on, 45–47

Fitzgerald, Mollie McQuillan, 90, 116

Fitzgerald, Scottie, 20, 36

Fitzgerald, Zelda Sayre, 20, 27, 88, 93, 94

Flappers, 88–90, 91, 93–96

Forster, E.M., 73–75

Franklin, Benjamin, 67–69

Frontier myth. See American Dream; Cody, Dan

G

Gatsby, Jay

  as advertising imagery rather than human, 55

  as American Dream embodiment, 23–25

  as American Everyman, 111–112

  consumerism and, 54–55

  as destroyed by very elements that enabled his rise, 109

  naiveté of, 100

  romantic nature of, 64–65

  romanticism v. values of, 65–66

  as self-invented man, 80–83

  as symbol of American dream born too late, 82–86

  as unable to survive in postwar class structure wasteland, 64–65

  as war hero, 48–49

Gatz, Jimmy. See Gatsby, Jay

Gotti, John, 233–238

Graham, Sheilah, 43, 51

The Great Gatsby (1974 film version), 34

The Great Gatsby (Fitzgerald)

  American history and, 72

  cars and driving in, 58

  as conveying clash of two American Dreams, 67–72

critical adulation for, 21–22

as criticism of American
Dream, 75–76

as demystifying the American
myth, 61–66

destruction created by modern technology in, 56–58

illusion v. reality in, 21–22

imagery of, 76–79, 90–91

as indictment of American
class system, 97–100

ironies of, 63, 109

literary techniques in, 76–79

metaphor in, 57–58

plot summmary, 18–20

restlessness v. stagnant nature
of upper class in, 64–65

as revealing Fitzgerald's own
aspirations and frustrations,
110–112

simile in, 56

as social study of broken society, 62–64

as study of carelessness, 108–
112

symbolism in, 62, 65, 68, 108,
112

tragedy of, 64

universality of themes of,
60–66

waste land metaphor in, 57–
58, 60, 62, 97

women of, 88, 90–92

writing of, 18

See also Specific characters

H

Hemingway, Ernest, 11, 51–52

Hilton, Paris, 128–129, *131*, 132

Howard's End (Forster), 73–75

Hynes, Samuel, 84

I

Irresponsibility, 108–112

J

Jazz Age. *See* 1920s

K

King, Ginevra, 18

L

The Last Tycoon (Fitzgerald), 51

Lee, David D., 49

Lord Jim (Conrad), 109

M

Mencken, H.L., 11

Milford, Nancy, 94

Moral complacency, 67–69, 70, 71

N

1920s
business and consumerism as
key value of, 32, 53–56

Fitzgerald on, 31, 32

money and virtue during,
33–34

social and cultural changes
during, 32

See also World War I

Nystrom, Paul, 56

P

Princeton University, 39–44

Prohibition, *77*

Protestantism, 83–84

R

Rapping, Elayne, 129–130

Recklessness, 108–112

Reed, John, 11

Religion, 83–84
"The Rich Boy" (Fitzgerald), 48

S

Saturday Evening Post, 54, 91
Schervish, Paul, 130–131
Seldes, Gilbert, 22
Self-reliance, 68–72
Sergeant York: An American Hero (Lee), 49
This Side of Paradise (Fitzgerald), 36, 37, 39, 43–44, 51
Socialism, 113–118
Socrates, 68
Sorority scandal, 139–144
"The Spire and the Gargoyle" (Fitzgerald), 37
Stern, Milton R., 50

T

Tender is the Night (Fitzgerald), 50, 95

Trilling, Lionel, 73, 111
Trump, Ivanka, 130

V

Victorian era, 84–85

W

Waste, 56–58
    See also Carelessness; Consumerism
The Waste Land (Eliot), 57–58, 62, 97
Wharton, Edith, 79
Wilson, Edmund, 34, 54, 89, 114
Wilson, George, 108
Wilson, Myrtle, 56, 58–59, 90, 96
Wolfsheim, Meyer, 76, 81, 133
Wood, Diane, 132
World War I, 49–51, *57*

Y

York, Alvin, 45, 49